QUEST FOR ANSWERS

Real People with Questions

GTStarr

*Ask, and it shall be given you; seek, and
ye shall find; knock and it shall be opened
unto you: (Mathew 7:7 KJV)*

CONTENTS

CHAPTERS OVERVIEW

Chapter 1

How can I find myself after leaving
the adult industry?

What do you do with your life if you're 30 years old
and have nothing to show in life, only mistakes?

Why don't I know who I am? I feel like
everything I do or say is fake and I don't know
if my problems are imaginary or not.

How could I move from the depth of
despair to the height of ecstasy?

How can I become more optimistic
after losing so much?

When frustrated, I have radical thoughts
about human society, our population, our
sustainability, and our impact on nature. Am I
alone? Am I evil? ... or just a psychopath?

Should I feel bad if I think my son should be better off dead then be a drug addict?

Chapter 2

How does self-awareness differ from enlightenment?

When has it ever struck you how lucky you are to be alive, and why? What happened to bring this realization to your awareness?

Chapter 3

What is one bad habit that almost (or did) ruined your life? How did you become aware of this habit? What did you do to get rid of it?

What is a behavior that confident and self-assured people do not exhibit?

Who sucks the air out of your life, and what are you doing to change that?

What behavioral characteristics make narcissists apt to resist changing their bad habits?

How does unhappiness lead to self-destructive behavior?

What are some bad habits to follow?

Chapter 4

What causes a person to have difficulty regulating their emotions?

How important are your emotions to yourself?

Why should adolescents learn how to manage their emotions?

Chapter 5

When Julia walks in her neighborhood, she notices litter and graffiti everywhere. The graffiti is colorful, but she doesn't like it. Sometimes she thinks about picking up the trash, but she doesn't want to touch it. What is the main problem for Julia?

How is it that a hypothetical caregiver's incessant pampering, on the one hand, as well as excessive criticism, on the other, albeit opposite styles, both often results in a child's developing narcissistic patterns of behavior?

Chapter 6

How does one stop experiences from influencing future events?

Who do you make the most sacrifices for?

How often do you do nothing?

What was it like to be raised by a perfectionist?

What do you do when your insecurities are starting to take over?

Why is it harder to be happy as you age?

What is the biggest obstacle to overcome in life?

What are the main causes of victim mentality?

How much rejection is required to experience pain and to doubt life's meaning?

When you are swamped and overwhelmed by life, how do you avoid falling into bad habits and avoidance behavior? What self-talk or thoughts do you use to push forward despite the significant challenges?

Who has gone from a normal situation to a catastrophic personal situation in less than 1 hour?

Who would you like to see sober?

How were you able to overcome a difficult life experience?

What do you think of when you read or hear "to make something out of nothing"?

What is an impossible thing you've thought of today?

How do you stop feeling scared because you're falling behind in life compared to your peers?

How can an individual psychologically overcome pride?

Chapter 7

What does it mean to organize life with integrity?

When a person who doesn't have any conscious at all does something immoral, can he or she

keep going on with it without any hesitation between time to time, without at least making some self-justification, why or why not?

Chapter 8

How do I disprove a fear of not being in the real world?

How much are you in control of your own perception?

Chapter 9

Who are you today?

Who's chasing you down?

How far do your thoughts randomly wander?

What is your "I lived through that" event?

What is the most embarrassing situation that you have woken up to?

Chapter 10

**When conclusions are made about life,
is that freeing or restrictive?**

**What do you think of the phrase
"Never underestimate yourself and
never overestimate others"**

**When most people you grew up with have
died, is there anything worth living for?**

Chapter 11

How dangerous is it to let people define themselves?

**Why do some people gravitate to fear in
the face of disaster, more so than seeking
an optimistic solution or hope?**

**Whenever I face danger or think that I am facing
a life-threatening situation I try to immediately
turn to my "real" me, try to become self-conscious
and "aware" of that moment. I think that by**

doing that I will survive it. Why is that?

What psychological tricks work on most people?

What's the best mindset to help
conquer a fear of taking risks?

What can't I get if I'm not as good as you?

What is a personality disorder?

What are the recovery rates of people
who suffer with BPD?

Where does selfishness come from? Do babies start
out equal in terms of 'self-focus' and how do life
experiences change that over time? Why does one
person look excessively inward to satisfying their
own wants while others seek empathetic service?

How long does it take you to get used
to things you don't like?

How does owning your own mistakes help to
build character and mental strength?

Chapter 12

Why does the United States keep building prisons if they aren't effective in preventing recidivism?

Why has so much aggressiveness become part of our daily lives?

Who is the most dangerous person that you have ever met or encountered?

How do you describe apathy?

How do I break barriers and not accept limits?

Why does it seem like humanity can't get a win lately?

How did people live and feel a few generations ago, when the "strong ego" was still common?

How are we always basically in "survival mode" even when we think we are not, and why is this true?

Chapter 13

What is the best way to live safely?

What are your short rules for a better life?

Chapter 14

How do I stop feeling scared? What are some calming techniques?

What is a useful life hack you can learn in five minutes?

INTRODUCTION:

Humankind is characterized by an innate curiosity and the desire to seek knowledge and understanding. While some individuals are more driven to expand their knowledge, others may have a diminished curiosity. However, wisdom always endures and is waiting to be uncovered. Regardless of one's level of inquisitiveness, questions about life and existence arise, whether they are profound or trivial. These questions hold significance and should be asked.

Individuals often have personal questions that they seek to answer. They may be looking for a solution to a problem, or they may want to gain a new perspective or a different reality. Some people want to hear other people's views and perspectives, as the truth is often subjective and multi-faceted. From a Christian faith-based perspective, this book explores various questions and provides answers based on research, experience, and daily interactions.

The quest for knowledge and understanding is a natural human instinct, and this book is a compilation of real questions posed by individuals on social media and the author's responses. The author has refined and improved these responses for publication, and has also included quotes from influential figures to provide additional insights into specific topics. The world has a profound impact on our opinions and beliefs, but our character and principles are shaped by God.

The author's aim is to provide valuable insights and entertain the reader with this work. This book is the first in an ongoing series, and it is his hope that this book will be of help and contain something of value for all who come across it.

CHAPTER I - ADVICE

How can I find myself after leaving the adult industry?

"You totally value and respect your body as you get older"—Jenny McCarthy

You have taken a significant step in finding yourself by leaving the adult industry. This is commendable as the industry is exploitative and does not prioritize the well-being of its participants or society as a whole. Engaging in degrading sexual acts perpetuates suffering, addiction, and further perversion. The negative effects of lust on one's mental health, relationships, and overall productivity are well documented and cannot be ignored.

To move forward, it is important not to judge yourself and to sever ties with anyone involved in the industry to avoid temptation. If anyone tries to pull you back into it, they may not have your best interests at heart. Consider seeking therapy or talking to trusted individuals about your experiences, as this can help alleviate any lingering emotions.

In order to maintain a clear mindset, sobriety may

be necessary, especially if addiction is a factor. Consider seeking help through 12-step programs or other forms of addiction recovery. Praying to a higher power can also bring comfort and solace.

It is normal to experience feelings of shame, guilt, and remorse, but it is important to remember that these experiences do not define you. Work on your mental health and focus on moving forward in a positive direction. Remember, you have control over your own path in life, and can choose to grow from your experiences.

What do you do with your life if you're 30 years old and have nothing to show in life, only mistakes?

"I have made many decisions that I probably shouldn't have made, but life is about making mistakes, learning and moving on"—Shamita Shetty

Life is about embracing change and acceptance as without these, it can be difficult to progress. Begin today by making gradual changes, focusing on the present moment and leaving the past to historians and the future to fortune tellers. The mind can distort reality, making past events seem more catastrophic than they truly were. This can lead to self-dwelling and self-pity, which are detrimental habits to break.

To improve your life, replace these habits with positive ones such as prayer, meditation, journaling, and self-reflection. Consider taking classes and surrounding yourself with supportive individuals. It is important to have a plan of action as failing to plan is equivalent to planning to fail.

It is easy to fall into the trap of complicating one's life, but remember that you still have a chance to make things right. Ask for God's help and guidance each morning and trust that the right people will be put in your life. At 39, I finally took control of my life life, and you have a decade ahead to start making positive changes. Keep moving forward and never give up hope.

Why don't I know who I am? I feel like everything I do or say is fake and I don't know if my problems are imaginary or not.

"Knowing yourself is the beginning of wisdom of all"—Aristotle

Your problems aren't imaginary because you obviously experience them and perhaps are in distress. I would like to acknowledge that the difficulties you are facing are real and deserving of attention and care. It is not uncommon in today's fast-paced and technologically advanced world for individuals to struggle with self-discovery and confusion.

It is important to avoid relying on mind-altering substances as they can worsen confusion and hinder self-discovery. If you are struggling with substance dependency, seeking support from a licensed professional is crucial. Alternatives such as 12-Step programs, which provide a structured and supportive environment for individuals facing similar issues, may also be helpful in your healing journey.

Feeling like you don't know who you are or that your actions and words are inauthentic is a common experience for many people. This can be caused by a variety of factors, including societal pressures, past experiences, and internal conflicts.

It's important to remember that everyone's sense of self is constantly evolving and that it's normal to question your identity at times. It may be helpful to engage in self-reflection and exploration activities, such as journaling or therapy, to better understand yourself and your experiences.

It's also important to differentiate between imaginary problems and real concerns. Imaginary problems often stem from excessive worry or fear, whereas real problems are those that have tangible impacts on your life. Seeking support from a mental health professional can help you sort through these feelings and determine the best course of action.

Remember, finding and knowing yourself takes time and self-discovery is a lifelong journey. Be kind to yourself and trust in the process.

How could I move from the depth of despair to the height of ecstasy?

"Sometimes when you're in a dark place you think you've been buried, but you've actually been planted"—Christine Caine

Moving from a state of despair to one of ecstasy requires a multi-faceted approach that addresses both the physical and emotional aspects of well-being. Here are some steps you can take to help make this transition:

Seek professional help: If you are experiencing intense feelings of despair, it's important to reach out for help. A mental health professional, such as a psychologist or therapist, can provide support and guidance as you work through your feelings.

Practice self-care: Engage in activities that promote physical and emotional well-being, such as exercise, meditation, and spending time in nature. Make sure to also eat a healthy diet, get adequate sleep, and limit exposure to stressful stimuli.

Connect with others: Spend time with friends and family

members who are supportive and positive. Participate in social activities and volunteer opportunities to broaden your social network and increase feelings of connection and purpose.

Cultivate gratitude: Take time each day to reflect on the things you are thankful for, no matter how small. This can help shift your focus from negative thoughts and emotions to positive ones.

Engage in positive activities: Pursue hobbies and interests that bring you joy and fulfillment. Find activities that challenge and inspire you, and set goals for yourself that are achievable and meaningful.

Mindfulness and meditation: Practice mindfulness and meditation regularly to quiet the mind and increase feelings of calm and inner peace.

It's important to keep in mind that the path from despair to ecstasy can be a journey, and it may not happen overnight. However, by taking steps to improve your well-being and build resilience, you can create a foundation for lasting happiness and fulfillment.

In many cases, detoxifying the brain from addictive substances and behaviors can improve overall well-being. This includes limiting exposure to things that have a negative impact on the brain, such as electronic devices, media, and unhealthy foods. Practicing mindfulness, prayer, and physical activity can also contribute to a better state of mind.

Excessive exposure to compulsive behaviors can lead to a depletion of neurotransmitters, including dopamine, and result in feelings of despair. By detoxifying the brain, growth hormones and neurotransmitters, such as endorphins, can be naturally boosted, leading to a sense of euphoria.

Although the concept of detoxifying the brain may be simple, it can be difficult to put into practice because of ingrained habits and behaviors. Intermittent fasting and reducing the window of food consumption can also help to release growth hormones and improve overall well-being, mood, and energy levels.

How can I become more optimistic after losing so much?

"Optimism is the faith that leads to achievement. Nothing can be done without hope and confidence"—Helen Keller

Dealing with loss and despair is a difficult process, and it's different for everyone. It can be especially challenging in recent times with the substantial losses many people have faced, including loss of loved ones, health, jobs, and the isolation imposed by world leaders.

To move towards a more positive outlook, I focus on surrounding myself with positive people and avoiding negative influences. I make an effort to stay away from negative media and engage in activities that bring me peace of mind.

The key to staying optimistic is to have an attitude of gratitude and to focus on the things and people in our lives that we have, rather than what we've lost or what we don't have. This requires effort, dedication, and a change in our attitudes and habits.

To improve my mental health, I also make time for activities such as meditation, journaling, and therapy. Writing things down and exploring different tools for mental health recovery, such as workbooks and videos, can be helpful too. It's important to find what works best for you and to be open to trying different things. Remember, healing is a journey that takes time, effort, and sacrifice, but it's worth it.

Moving from a place of loss and despair to one of optimism can be challenging, but it is possible. Here are some things you can try:

Surround yourself with positive people: Seek out relationships with people who have a positive outlook on life and who support and encourage you.

Limit exposure to negative news and media: Avoid

consuming news and media that is excessively negative, as it can have a detrimental effect on your mental state.

Practice gratitude: Make a conscious effort to focus on what you have, rather than what you've lost, and be thankful for the people and things in your life.

Engage in self-care activities: This can include meditation, journaling, and exercising. Taking care of your mental and physical health can help improve your overall outlook on life.

Talk to a therapist: If your loss has left you feeling overwhelmed, consider speaking to a mental health professional who can help you work through your emotions and develop coping strategies.

Practice mindfulness: Pay attention to your thoughts and emotions, and try to stay present in the moment. This can help you avoid getting caught up in negative thinking patterns.

Remember, it's important to be patient and kind to yourself during this process. Rebuilding a positive outlook on life takes time, effort, and dedication, but it is possible.

When frustrated, I have radical thoughts about human society, our population, our

sustainability, and our impact on nature. Am I alone? Am I evil? ... or just a psychopath?

"If you so choose, every mistake can lead to greater understanding and effectiveness. If you so choose, every frustration can help you to be more patient and more persistent"— Ralph Marston

No, you are not inherently evil or a psychopath. It is common to experience negative and sometimes evil thoughts, but it is important to differentiate those thoughts from actions. Negative thinking can easily escalate and lead to negative emotions, which in turn drive behavior, relationships, and experiences. A peaceful and serene state of mind can bring about heaven on earth, but when the mind is consumed by chaos and turmoil, it can also lead to a feeling of hell.

Frustration stems from a lack of inner peace and calmness. A key step towards finding serenity is accepting and practicing patience. When we have high expectations of others, it often leads to decreased serenity. On the other hand, having low expectations of the world and those around us can lead to increased feelings of peace and tranquility. Remember, it's crucial to accept the world as it is and not attempt to control anyone other than ourselves.

Being a psychopath is a result of a combination of genetic and environmental factors, and it is not a choice. It's important to understand that having psychopathic tendencies or traits doesn't make someone evil or dangerous. However, if a person with psychopathic traits lacks the ability to empathize with others, they can engage in harmful behavior. It's crucial for individuals to seek help if they are struggling with antisocial behavior or harmful thoughts and to work on developing empathy and compassion. Additionally, it's essential for society to provide support and resources for those with psychopathic tendencies to help them lead a healthy and fulfilling life.

Psychopaths lack the ability to feel fear, which can make them braver than others in certain situations. In demanding fields that require courage and difficult decision-making, they may excel, especially if they have strong moral principles. It's important to remember that given the right circumstances and triggers, anyone is capable of acting in evil ways. Self-care and emotional regulation are crucial, as emotions play a major role in human motivation and drive most of our decisions, aside from deeply held beliefs and values.

Intimate relationships, careers, friendships, hobbies, and even the quality of life are all greatly influenced by one's emotions. Lust, love, motivation, and likings are the driving forces behind these choices. Selfishness or selflessness also stem from one's emotions and self-perception. A healthy emotional state is key to a longer and happier life, as chronic stress and frustration can harm both physical and mental well-being. While emotions play a significant role, it's important to remember that actions are not solely determined by them. Cultivating peace and serenity within oneself can lead to a more fulfilling life.

Should I feel bad if I think my son should be better off dead then be a drug addict?

"There are all kinds of addicts, I guess. We all have pain. And we all look for ways to make the pain go away"—Sherman Alexie

Addiction is a devastating mental illness that affects not only the individual struggling with it but also those close to them, particularly mothers. The pain it causes is immense and often leads to feelings of anger and frustration as part of the grieving process. Whether the addict is still alive or has passed away, the effects of addiction are far-reaching and impact everyone involved. My thoughts are with those who are facing this difficult situation.

The journey towards self-healing involves embracing your emotions, no matter how difficult they may be, with compassion and without judgment. Instead of denying or suppressing your feelings, it's important to acknowledge them, process them, and move forward at your own pace. Having an addicted loved one is a tough experience and it affects not only the individual but also their family. It's important to remember that addiction is a disease and that the person suffering is not themselves, but rather, a victim of its grip. If you have tried to help, know that you have done your best. Addiction is a family disease and it takes a toll on everyone involved.

Writing a letter to your son about his addiction may bring you some peace and closure, even if it doesn't change his situation. Expressing your feelings and concerns in a clear and heartfelt manner can help you process and come to terms with what's happening. It's important to remember that ultimately, your son's choices and actions are his own, and you can only do your best to support and help. However, if he's not ready to change, you may need to accept that and focus on moving forward with your own life.

It is not uncommon to feel overwhelmed and frustrated with a loved one's addiction, and these thoughts and feelings may seem unbearable. However, it is not healthy or appropriate to wish death upon someone, even if they are struggling with addiction, but at the same time it is quite understandable.

It is understandable to feel overwhelmed and hopeless in the face of your son's struggles. However, it's important to remember that he's is a human being with value and worth, regardless of his current situation. Rather than focusing on thoughts of death or harm, it might be more helpful to channel your energy towards finding resources and support for both yourself and your son. Seeking therapy or support groups for families of those struggling with addiction can be a helpful step towards finding a healthier and more compassionate approach to the situation.

Additionally, reaching out to addiction treatment facilities and resources can help you understand the options available for your son's recovery. Remember, addiction is a disease and the best way to support your loved one is through compassion and seeking help for them and for yourself.

CHAPTER II - AWARENESS

How does self-awareness differ from enlightenment?

"To enjoy good health, to bring true happiness to one's family, to bring peace to all, one must first discipline and control one's own mind. If a man can control his mind he can find the way to Enlightenment, and all wisdom and virtue will naturally come to him"—Buddha

Self-awareness is a heightened sense of self-understanding that involves a deeper examination of one's thoughts, behaviors, and emotions. It allows individuals to recognize and understand their motivations and drives, and to make changes or improvements if necessary. With self-awareness, individuals are better equipped to make conscious choices about their lives and to maintain a sense of control over their own emotions and experiences.

Enlightenment is a state of being in which one has a deep sense of acceptance and peace with oneself, characterized by the declaration "I AM". It brings with it a sense of serenity, joy, and gratitude, regardless of past or present circumstances. This state of enlightenment is achieved through conscious connection with the divine, the universe, or the world, and involves a lack of judgment or suffering over the way things are. It is a state of flowing with life, embracing it as it is, without resistance.

When has it ever struck you how lucky you are to be alive, and why? What happened to bring this realization to your awareness?

"I am grateful for who I am and who I am not. I am grateful for the life I have been given and for all that I have and all that I don't. Every breath I take is a blessing and an opportunity to fully experience the sheer joy of being alive"—Miranda Kerr

I suppose my Near Death Experience (NDR) made me aware my life is a bonus round. This experience also gave me realization I should no longer take life for granted and coupled with other factors my outlook on life finally changed. Not all the time and it comes and goes because I'm not self-aware all the time when I'm going through life's motions. It's sort of like- I realize I still exist and I can experience everything with a fresh set of eyes. That adds a new layer because time is limited.

Another thing is the following. Sooner or later, we are all going to die folks and there isn't any ifs and buts about it. Everyone of us is going to face the Creator. I believe that today more than ever and an account of the life we led has to be given. The book of life, also know as the bible talks about it all. BIBLE also stands for BASIC INSTRUCTION BEFORE LEAVING EARTH. It's a manual for living and contains universal truths, mistakes of others and warnings. It also contains revelations of things to come.

Awareness and enlightenment provide a chance to realize who is in charge and enable personal change before the time runs out, repent and turn to God. And it's not going to be pretty for most people, I believe. I don't want to scare people, but I'm scared of God. No one can go to heaven on their own merit because they believe they're good people. That's the deception and the delusion of the human mind.

This is what I believe and I'm not here to throw my beliefs unto the world, but I want people to be aware of that. This is what my life led me to because of my experiences. It took me down this path. And I'm sorry if I make others uncomfortable but that is the truth as I see it today. I'm not a holy roller but a regular dude with problems and it makes sense to me that nothing created itself out of nowhere, hence there is a God and judgment after death. People need to accept Jesus Christ as their Lord and savior and not rely on their own goodness.

CHAPTER III – BEHAVIORS AND HABITS

What is one bad habit that almost (or did) ruined your life? How did you become aware of this habit? What did you do to get rid of it?

"It is easier to prevent bad habits than to break them"—Benjamin Franklin

My addiction almost ruined my life. It robbed me of peace of mind, happy life, health and it destroyed many great relationships with other people. It hurt me and it injured others in my path. Some people, such as my family and those close to me, suffered more. I am not proud of my actions and behaviors. Addiction incapacitated me as well. Let me correct myself: I did all that to myself.

Addiction gives at first. It promised me the sky and it gave me the wings to fly. I did fly for a while. I had a great time at some point in my life in its infancy. I can not say that it was all dull and painful. No. It was an experience that I will never forget- both awesome but later mostly painful and full of suffering. The lie is that fun and good time can be maintained but that is the farthest from the truth and it will be replaced by pain. In this case, pain is mandatory but suffering is optional. It is up to a person in the grips of addiction how long they will suffer. I chose to suffer while I didn't have to.

Addiction gave me the wings, but it took away the sky. The fall was hard and nearly deadly. Addiction should be avoided like a plague. It will decimate anything and everything in its path. It is the cause of society's ills and troubles to a great extent and many people are affected, not just a person using. Addiction alters entire generations and is considered a family disease.

How did I become aware of it? I knew that a problem existed for a long time and so did people in my life. The consequences were obvious and I could no longer go about my life letting this rule me. It was bigger than I. I was small and it towered over me and ruled my life, chipping away at my soul, mind, and body until it had what it wanted. It had me in its grip and it squeezed the life out of me until I literally could no longer breathe. It had me and I became a slave to master more powerful than any king or authority figure. My drug became my God. That is very dangerous, and many addicts do not think that they have a problem or they convince themselves that they can stop any time. It is true. Addict can stop any time, but for how long? That is the million dollar question. The obsession of the mind almost always returns; guaranteed—without the Higher Power.

I sought help and did something about it. I was once a victim and today I am the executioner. I execute my plans and life the way I see fit. Not the way my master tells me to. I work on myself every day and I am available to others. By getting out of myself, I can focus on others. I can also focus on myself because today I love myself and I love life and I feel good about myself. My self-esteem and self-respect returned from the land of the living dead. They were on vacation of a lifetime, unfortunately.

Addiction is a matter of life or death. You either stay busy living or stay busy dying. The choice is yours. I choose life. Life OR Death. I was spared to carry the message. If I don't want to be a message, I have to carry it. Besides, I'm very passionate about recovery ever since I got sober. I want to get better with life and I know others can and will recover if priority is assigned to recovery. Please seek help if a challenge of such magnitude exists. It gets better and it's possible to heal with honesty, openmindedness and willingness to do the work.

What is a behavior that confident and self-assured people do not exhibit?

"Confidence comes from discipline and training"—Robert Kiyosaki

What I can state about confident behavior is the following: Confident people don't need to be on social media constantly posting things to be noticed. A person doesn't need to do things or say things for the validation of others because they know their worth. They don't have to stay quiet if they have something to say, but may choose not to say anything, anyway. Confident people don't walk around slouched or with head hung low, looking for coins to pick up on the ground all day long. They have no need to be controlling and aggressively assertive, or constantly reserved for people to respect them.

They don't have to dominate conversations or brag about stuff for the purpose of looking self-assured or do anything at all. They don't even have to play or watch popular sports just because everyone else around them does if that's not what they're into. Confident people don't have to go to the gym and work out four days a week in order to maintain perfect body and draw confidence from their physical appearance, although I'm sure that helps. They don't have to have the prettiest girl or the cutest guy in order to feel fulfilled or show off in a sports car if the only goal is to impress someone; look to external things for their confidence. Confidence can be drawn from God who builds people up. Confident people look in the eye when talking, with head held straight a good posture. What solidifies a confident person is a firm and solid handshake. Confident person has enough humility to recognize that the other person is a human being and no one is better or worse than anyone else. That kind of person takes the day as it comes without forcing it upon the world.

**Who sucks the air out of your life, and
what are you doing to change that?**

*"Giving up smoking is easy. I've done it
a hundred times…"*—Mark Twain

I suck the air out of my life literally — I did. I'm killing the old me and that's the best thing I can do for myself. I've quit smoking and that sucked the air of my lungs and money out of my pockets first off without going deeper into a rabbit hole of things and a lifestyle that almost killed me. Anyone that smokes should seriously consider doing something about it— God could and would help, if God was sought. As far as people go, I stay away from negative influences as much as I'm able to. In most cases, I found that the issue is me, since I have much control regarding the environment I find myself in.

**What behavioral characteristics make narcissists
apt to resist changing their bad habits?**

*"Love doesn't die a natural death.
Love has to be killed, either by neglect
or narcissism"*— Frank Salvato

Narcissists may not be aware they have a problem because everyone else is at fault. It's always someone else's fault and if narcissists are aware of the detrimental behavior, they may not care because rationalizations and justification obstruct sound reasoning and it depends if they're malignant people or not. But one behavioral characteristic may be a predatory stare that makes others uncomfortable and may be a result of living in a fantasy land and objectifying people that they're attracted to, for example, or just asserting their dominance in a crowd/ sociopaths. Another behavior could be a display of impatience in public, like waiting in line and throwing a tantrum because the line doesn't move too fast. They may not be apt at changing that because they're easily aggravated, unable to contain themselves about anything that stops them from their day without consideration for others. Impatient and in a hurry.

I saw a narcissist buy cigarettes and a drink and pay with a card tap. He tapped the card on the screen and walked out right away in some elastic workout gear like he was ready for a marathon with a cigarette in his mouth, but forgot to initiate the tap payment. The register person knocked on the window and called him over. He rushed in and when told that he needed to tap the payment, the dude just lost it. Blamed everything on the register person.

"You did something"- he said and after some exchange, threw the smokes and a drink, said he doesn't want it- "It's your fault." Like . . . whatever dude. Now you gotta go somewhere else for the smokes and a drink. You're not doing yourself a favor at all and only hurt yourself. Stay away from these charmers, everyone.

How does unhappiness lead to self-destructive behavior?

"When we meet real tragedy in life, we can react in two ways - either by losing hope and falling into self-destructive habits, or by using the challenge to find our inner strength. Thanks to the teachings of Buddha, I have been able to take this second way"—Dalai Lama

Destruction because of unhappiness happens very easy. Unhappy people are not fulfilled. What are they missing? There is a huge void and emptiness inside that needs to be filled. It's filled with relationships that may not necessarily be healthy, but rather destructive. It's filled with addiction, fueled by binges, and there are plenty of those around . . . binges and different addictions. That alone always goes with destructive and dangerous behavior, as it's naturally a self-destructive path. For instance, you cop drugs to support the habit right? Now you have to deal with drug dealers, shady interactions and the police on the other side of the spectrum. It's all open to imagination of what that leads to and nothing related to that lifestyle is healing.

Eating habits are detrimental as well when people are unhappy. They eat for comfort and to quell negative emotions that includes their pain, suffering and unfulfilled lives. On top of that, many people use food alone as a drug to medicate themselves and their unhappy circumstances. That leads to detrimental health issues and challenges not limited to obesity, inflammations, diabetes.

Unhappiness may be filled with constantly seeking something and being unable to go on in the late stages of unhappiness, experiencing doom and gloom. Some people just feel like they have no way out and speed up the process of doom. Some people self-harm in a variety of ways to relieve those feelings because pain is so great and self-harm bring temporary relief.

There are lots of aggression associated with unhappiness and that too has dire consequences for everyone involved. I can't see how happy people act that way, rather those that look to escape themselves will probably be more chaotic and troublesome.

Some people shut down and isolate. That's very destructive and unhealthy behavior too. Others seek notoriety and validation. For some, bad reputation still gets them the attention they crave. Underneath, it's all fear based. People cheat more often when they're unhappy. Maybe they were never happy in the first place with their relationship. Or maybe they just don't give a thought about it and are wired to be that way.

Psychopaths and malignant people could just be constructed that way, I guess. But psychopathy isn't one fit all. Some are more principled that most inhabitants of the blue planet. Some people play God too, driven by never fulfilled urges, desires and reptilian compulsive brains. A lot can be said about situational unhappiness It's an umbrella term for many things.

What are some bad habits to follow?

"My wife is amazing. She had to know she was getting into a heap of trouble when we met"—Taylor Hanson

Spend more money if you can and buy an American if you live in that country. Anywhere you live on the planet, support your community and enterprises instead of the lie of globalism that we have recently witnessed emerging in recent years. That's one bad money habit I'd like to follow myself because if people live in the community, they ought to buy locally, even if it costs more.

Society has to learn how to be self sufficient again and to rely back on local economy ; to do things ourselves. The same thing goes for everyone else. Global society became a failure and the post COVID impact proves it unequivocally when countries have to rely on other countries for goods and services while the whole system and supply chain has been disrupted. When the restrictions were implemented and logistical issues arouse, it became hard to get what is needed. Everything comes to a hold and more people are affected than ever before because the global interconnectedness.

CHAPTER IV-EMOTIONS

What causes a person to have difficulty regulating their emotions?

"When you're busy blocking out difficult emotions and feelings, you're not going to feel the good stuff, either"—Valerie Bertinelli

The number 1 offender is likely resentment—People, places, things which trigger destructive emotions. It originates through the thinking program acquired/downloaded in the first years of life from the surroundings. It may be accompanied by genetic predisposition as well. Sometimes, triggers are activated unconsciously—could be driven by shame instilled in childhood that activates strong negative feelings.

Other times, it has to do with thought distortions and the belief systems that reinforce those emotions. Mostly mental illness triggers difficulty regulating emotions. For example, people with ADHD and ADD-attention deficit disorder are proven to get frustrated much quicker and faster than those who lack trouble focusing. People with Borderline Personality Disorder have a very difficult time regulating their emotions because in some individuals trauma and neglect was present at the young age. Children find ways to cope with the emotional pain in unhealthy ways and often those emotions persist for longer periods of time, even after the smoke from a heated interaction clears. They are quicker to react to perceived attacks or injustice towards them and they experience the emotions on a deeper level, in both ways.

Emotions are also addictive and that's a fact. People take comfort in what feels natural and there is little defense against them, other than recognizing one's triggers and incorporating counter measures and healthy coping skills through awareness and practice— namely behavior and thinking modification as well as, perhaps most importantly—spiritual fitness.

How important are your emotions to yourself?

"Emotional intelligence is the ability to sense, understand, and effectively apply the power and acumen of emotions as a source of human energy, information, connection, and influence"—Robert K. Cooper, PhD

One of the most important thing in the world to me are my emotions. I want to know everything there is to know about them and how to handle them properly. It may sound selfish, but it is nothing but selfish. It is self-care of the highest order. Improper experience of emotions caused me so much pain, heartache and challenges in life that it would take a book to explain it properly. Others are also affected as well.

I care about myself and I care about the world around me. I'm a sensitive person and that insight and self-awareness encourages me to work on and guard against certain emotions. So yes! My emotions are very important to me. If I don't have a grip on my emotions, I don't have anything anyway, because true happiness lies inside emotional well being. It is not a filled by status, accomplishment or the material world. Sure it all helps, but that kind of approach is meaningless in itself. Nothing matters because if emotions control me and I no longer have an upper hand in my own life, I drift into the universe like a lost comet.

I also accept my emotions because creation doesn't make mistakes, yet proper channeling is as relevant. Fear!!! Face everything and recover. Not fear everything and run. I used to run all the time because fear was a strong emotion in me, even I portrayed a false bravado and destructive behavior.

Why should adolescents learn how to manage their emotions?

"Care for your psyche...know thyself, for once we know ourselves, we may learn how to care for ourselves"—Socrates

Emotions are the most significant aspect of a person's experiences because everything revolves around them. Their proper management should happen as soon as children and youth are consciously aware of them as learning occurs early on. Children know what makes them joyous or sad, however, more complex emotions are hard to pinpoint and understand, and deal with.

Adolescents experience significant changes on several levels, including physiological and cognitive processes, and it affects everything about them, especially emotions. Emotions may overwhelm minors as they navigate new surrounding, explore themselves and each other, and potent feelings arise out of them. Adolescents also rebel and challenge authority as hormones change and alter their neuro-chemical pathways. They are also highly creative and idealistic force with the feelings guiding them. Some children are more sensitive. For these adolescents, life can be extremely challenging and unbearable. It's thus necessary to learn and handle them the right way, before they spiral out of control and cause harm.

Feelings and emotions guide a lot of thinking. These reinforce a variety of behavioral patterns. It is important to understand and properly experience emotions because based on these emotions, connections, alliances, isolations and perceptions form. Feelings alter the entire outlook in either direction. Emotions are responsible for loving a parent or having resentments towards them or others. They increase blissfulness or bring out despondency and anxiety. Emotions can build relationships and can also destroy them. Simply stated, life and death begin with emotions if wrong choices are made based on them. Sorrow and joy are born out of them and since juveniles sometimes cannot think critically or comprehend certain issues until adulthood, they rely on feelings.

Life wouldn't be worth living without emotions. They compose of simple and complex when experienced because feelings at the moment may initiate from the past—memories. Adolescents may have even more difficulties discerning emotions because of already mentioned changes taking place and much less experience with life. They can easily make wrong judgment calls, as well as action based on judging themselves and the lens through which they perceive the world around them. They want to fit in, but the external factors can be harsh. It's a fine art balancing emotional health.

Adults make many wrong judgment calls as well. Most adults can't always diagnose every one of them, either. No one is immune to emotions. All of us make choices based on how we feel. These emotions can decide the faith of the rest of our lives in terms of how it unfolds, however, adolescents are much more vulnerable. They explore who they are and what they like in that stage of development. They haven't developed a solid personality and character yet, and therefore, the ability to control emotions is underdeveloped as well. The earlier one learns how to manage emotions, the more benefits and fruitful living in years to come.

CHAPTER V - HYPOTHETICAL

When Julia walks in her neighborhood, she notices litter and graffiti everywhere. The graffiti is colorful, but she doesn't like it. Sometimes she thinks about picking up the trash, but she doesn't want to touch it. What is the main problem for Julia?

"Be the change you want to see in the world"—Ghandi

Julia doesn't have a problem. People who graffiti and litter have a big problem on the other hand. It takes more than one person to fix her neighborhood, but it does have to start somewhere. Julia also probably wants to pass the buck to someone else, but the problem won't fix itself.

My very good friend lives in one of those neighborhoods. I went to see him once, and he was in the middle of it all, picking the trash and cleaning the neighborhood. He took action when he saw a problem. He didn't hang out with me and say:
"G . . . this neighborhood is a mess. I wish things were different here, you know!"

That kind of talk and thinking will leave you blue

in the face and still nothing would change. This great dude took action and he inspired me as well. He once told me: "I want to leave this place better than I found it" What a profound statement. Him and I and number of people in his neighborhood had a community effort to clean the neighborhood on Saturday. The neighborhood had a lot of dumped trash over the years and it was a mess. My friend organized the whole event with the city and later after we cleaned the area, a city trash truck arrival. We helped the sanitation squad get rid of everything that sat on the pavement and made a huge difference in the neighborhood. My friend organized these events multiple times.

What is the problem you ask? Wishful thinking is the problem. Wishing things were better is just that, while sitting on the couch eating potato chips. It's all that and a bag of empty chips on the sidewalk now. Julia's problem is being in 95% of the population. The odds are stacked against her and the community that expects someone else to do something about it.

How is it that a hypothetical caregiver's incessant pampering, on the one hand, as well as excessive criticism, on the other, albeit opposite styles, both often results in a child's developing narcissistic patterns of behavior?

"The mother gazes at the baby in her arms, and the baby gazes at his mother's face and finds

himself therein...provided that the mother is really looking at the unique, small, helpless being and not projecting her own expectations, fears, and plans for the child. In that case, the child would find not himself in his mother's face, but rather the mother's own projections. This child would remain without a mirror, and for the rest of his life would be seeking this mirror in vain"—Donald Woods Winnicott

Pampering leads to entitlement and that leads to "I deserve to have that. I shouldn't have to work hard at it. I am better qualified. I should run this place" or, "Look at me. Look what I can do. I work so hard and I'm better than you," which may be true but stems from low self-worth and may lead to over-achieve at the expense of others because it's about the competition and own self-inadequacy.

Vanity is a vice. It is excessive pride in one's own abilities and appearance. Pampering gets a person things without working for them and without appreciating them fully. It spoils people who have things handed to them on a golden spoon.

"Perhaps because I don't appreciate them, I see little value in them. Because I see little value in them, I also see little value in people." Both people and objects can be easily discarded and replaced by the very nature of distorted thinking in progress:

"I don't need you. I can do this on my own and better. You are hindering and suffocating me. I can find someone who can understand me better. I know I am superficial, but that's just how it is." A sexist narcissist can thus objectify individuals, both women and men, in a lustful way. It's about fulfillment of their own selfish desires and undermines the uniqueness of the other individuals, their emotions and need.

"I can't connect on a deeper level and thus I speak love with my mouth and carnal fascination. That is how I show my connection." It is a sickness of the mind, body, soul, and spirit. Such individual know that true contentment hinges on proper relationships with each other and the world. They don't have that and inside they despise themselves.

"I want to romantically lust after you and I want to be lusted after. So I'm married but I can't help myself" It is another form of a drug that fills the emptiness, fuels the void, selfishness, egotism, egoism, self-centeredness, and selfishness disguised as caring. Excessive criticism leads to ego-mania with an inferiority complex.

"I judge myself as not good enough but yet with fewer flaws than you" Because I was criticized, I feel on edge when I am being corrected by you. I'm not listening. I'm not even hearing from you right now. You are attacking me. Because I am being corrected or rebuked by you, I feel like I am being judged. Because I feel like I am being judged by you, I judge myself. Because I feel inadequate, I no longer run on reason, but emotions such as anger and frustration take over and now that leads to gas-lighting and blaming you. I am burning the house down."

Anger inevitably leads to diminished empathy for another individual because a person with narcissistic traits has little empathy for themselves, in the first place. Since they have little empathy for themselves, they may or may not self-destruct with alcohol and narcotics.

They wreak havoc in the lives of others by default until they mend their ways and realize the self-destructive nature and behavior is unacceptable. It happens through self-awareness, if they're able to have honesty, open-mindedness and willingness to change and not be too far gone. Without that, little, if any, progress will ever be made. A certain degree of humility is also required in order to achieve the ability to change. Self-awareness and knowing that a challenge exists is the key and the pain must be greater than acceptable rewards to the behaviors being constantly reinforced.

"Yes. It happened during childhood. Parents criticized or pampered me. Now I have a responsibility to become a decent human being and make things right. I am the problem here, not anyone else. Wow! What a revelation. I guess I'm not the director on the stage of the world affairs after all, but only an actor. I ought to stick to the right script, fall back in line and tame my ego a bit; stay in my own lane and not regulate or control anyone but myself."

CHAPTER VI - MENTAL CHALLENGES

How does one stop experiences from influencing future events?

"When we are tired, we are attacked by ideas we conquered long ago"—Friedrich Nietzsche.

It's not always possible to simply overcome the influence of the past on the future events. However, many things help. Peace of mind is contingent on good rest. When something significant and noteworthy occurs, only self-reflection afterwards may bring future progress, along with keeping a journal and writing about it to reinforce the situation and learning.

Talking about and getting a feedback from someone who understands what going on provides an insight to focus on and work through. Also, being aware of it and accepting it. Surrender helps promote change. Some kind of behavior modification also should take place—a form of recovery. Trial and error and progress through time, experience and God— perhaps in the first place.

Asking God for help in overcoming those instance.

God is very underrated because people usually try to fix everything themselves and not rely on anyone but themselves. Stop trying and start relying on God ought to be the correct attitude. It's the pride that causes most human downfall and begets all the problems of the world.

Who do you make the most sacrifices for?

"We can never obtain peace in the outer world until we make peace with ourselves" —Buddha

I make the most sacrifice for my peace of mind. It costs a lot of time and effort. It's not easy, but most things worthy of improvement take commitment. If it was easy, everyone would be doing it and many people don't to that enough in order to ensure enhanced well-being.

I speak of myself as well. In the past that was precisely my attitude. It's clear society is getting sicker year by year. Priorities are in the wrong place. It took me years to finally start making lasting changes in my own life and therefore I understand self-improvement is one of the most difficult things at first. I wouldn't call myself healed, with oscillating days, but life's pressing forward in a better direction when everything is magnified and I look at the big picture, where I was and where I am now. I'm learning much these days about my own nature and deficiencies.

How often do you do nothing?

"The results you achieve will be in direct proportion to the effort you apply"— Denis Waitley

Rarely. I always do something—only when I meditate I do nothing. But even then I think too much. I'm high performance; sometimes I over think it. I used to be ADHD. Now I'm working on ADD. That's a joke. My disorder is an asset, especially when I write and knowing that helps me channel my mental challenges in the right direction.

What was it like to be raised by a perfectionist?

"Progress not perfection… you can't be perfect everything… but you can gain progress on a daily basis"—Court McGee

It's tough on everyone. Perfectionism is a common neurosis and many people are sufferers of it and affected, including me. On top of that, the virus infects others—notably children. Care givers way too often know what's best for their offspring or so they conjure up in their minds without realizing individual's unique drives, gifts and potential talents or set of interests that need fire to be lit under instead of pushing them into rebellion. Unfortunately, parents have their upbringing issues and Marix moments were engrained biases and cognitive dissonance moments flare up, and cloud their judgment.

What do you do when your insecurities are starting to take over?

"Despite the natural belittling of one's self, the doubts, the insecurities, we have to wake up to the realization that we all write our own autobiography, we are the authors of our life story. Realizing that, write a good story with your life and make sure to write yourself as the protagonist. Be the hero of your journey"—Yossi Ghinsberg

Rest, journal, talk about it, pray about it, recovery about it—including service to others, because insecurities result from dwelling on myself or my situation and falling into victimhood or self-pity mentality. Avoid falling into JARS.

J-A-R-S is a big one—Don't fall into it.

Jealousy of others and comparing oneself to the life of someone else is a definite barrier to self-compassion promotes more insecurities. Never compare yourself to anyone else. Everyone got things and challenges going on in life no matter how good things may look on the outside. That's your journey, so compare yourself to yourself and the progress you make.

Anger is a human emotion and therefore normal to a degree if it's not acted upon in a destructive manner. However, when anger turns to rage it's very unhealthy and destructive because insecurities won over. The control has been lost and emotions dictate further thoughts and behaviors resulting in more danger to oneself and others.

Resentment is anything that causes disturbances for too long and it isn't good nor healthy. Insecurities may initiate resentment to people, places and things. It is one of the most destructive and unhealthy emotions causing personal dissatisfaction. One ought to discover what's going on and work through it. That's a huge one because it leads to the "I don't cares" and isolation, more isolation and more issues.

Self-pity is also very, if not the most wasteful emotion when it comes to insecurities. "I'm the victim and poor me. My life is over," type of attitude. "Things and life is messed up, I'll never get better," and slew of other issues. All these are very dangerous as I have learned and experienced in my own journey to get rid of insecurities.

Keep the lid on the JARS—TURN TO YOUR HIGHER POWER and others for support. Join a recovery group, church, volunteer your time and services and be part of something bigger than yourself—God JESUS is the solution.

Why is it harder to be happy as you age?

"What we choose to focus on and what we choose to ignore—plays in defining the quality of our life"— Cal Newport

There is a reason why children are a lot happier than the aging population. In youth, people feel unstoppable. They're young, resilient, naïve many times and they bounce back quicker from what life throws at them. They lack the responsibilities and fear of the adult life.

They still trust things will be alright long term, discounting the unfortunate instances in which children suffer too — intense trauma, abuse or loss, perhaps. Also, children are about people and connection, while financial issues are generally a big issue later on in life when it comes to unhappiness or unfulfilled lives.

Children are a lot more adventure and curious, which loses its potency as individuals age out and become more concrete. That includes more friends and social life and dreams of finding one's place in the world. They may still have dreams and goals and feel like they have plenty of time to accomplish them—finish a good school and get a great paying job they'll love forever, for instance. It's also a difficult time of transition without adequate guidance but generally children are joyous and excited with what life brings.

Then stuff happens. You realize it might have been a lie or life as you picture wasn't destined for you. Perhaps many wrong choice culminated in unhappiness

Maybe you married the wrong person,
Maybe someone betrayed you,

Maybe you lost a best friend or a family member,
Maybe you put your priorities in the wrong people, place and things, and now it shows,
Maybe you never got the job you wanted or you hate the job you have,
Maybe you don't have a job and wish you did because of some circumstances holding you back,
Maybe you just lost your house because the bank took it away,
Maybe the fear holds you back and stops you from living life the way you would like to,
Maybe . . . Fill in the blank. Anything can be an issue if people let it be an issue. People usually focus on what they lack in life instead being grateful for what they do have.

Maybe happiness is not what we think it is, and look for it in wrong places. Maybe people became their own gods, but know not such is the case and the true connection with the ultimate God is missing!

What is the biggest obstacle to overcome in life?

"Success is to be measured not so much
by the position that one has reached
in life as by the obstacles which he has
overcome"—Booker T. Washington

The biggest obstacle to overcome in life is oneself because of innate fear. Fear is to FACE EVERYTHING AND RECOVER—not fear everything and run because the going gets tough. The first instinct is usually to give up and doubt one's ability to overcome the challenge and quit before the miracle happens.

For me anyway, the biggest obstacle to overcome is myself—the nagging self-sabotage inside telling me I'm not good enough or worthy of having it, or my emotional inconsistency. It has lessened since I'm actively participating in changing my circumstances and growing beyond it. It's a life-long process and needs to continue because it works better when a person is actively seeking betterment.

What are the main causes of victim mentality?

"I am not a victim of emotional conflicts.

I am human"—Marilyn Monroe

Main causes of victim mentality are trauma, abuse, neglect, mistreatment, negative childhood experiences. The biggest causes of victim mentality is being stuck in the past hurts and not growing beyond it. Victim mentality often assigns blame and troubles onto others. The person was wronged or feels wronged by actions of someone else and because of that experience there is often a sense of justified anger or righteous indignation.

Victim mentality causes strong emotions and prevents growth. There is a sense of feeling that the person is flawed and unwell and therefore uses that excuse not to move forward in life. Victim mentality hold people back because resentments are deeply engrained—and resentment is number one offender in life and is self-destructive.

IIow much rejection is required to experience pain and to doubt life's meaning?

"Rejection is merely a redirection; a course correction to your destiny"—Bryant McGill

I'm not sure how much rejection would be required to doubt life's meaning. Pain could be experienced with little rejection, for anyone. Some kind of pain, that is.

Rejection is part of life and happens to everyone. People get rejected all the time, whether it be applying for a job without desired result, not getting a second date; not getting a date altogether, or not getting into a dream school, for example. People get shut down all the time by someone or something because they didn't qualify for something or someone else had better connections. Even unanswered prayers can feel like rejection (wrong prayers by the way) from God and feeling unworthy in the presence of the Almighty.

Most people move on without too much difficulty, because rejection wasn't strong in their lives and they have strong support to sustain that blow. It blows over. Some people get rejected because they push too hard and they have to get rejected. They won't always get what they want and it teaches people they can't have everything they want.

If I had to mention about rejection, I'd say that it depends how much a child was rejected or believed, rejection occurred. Because if it occurred a lot, or was perceived a lot, then even a small amount of perceived rejection later in life, can uproot stability for the moment, or even days.

Rejection activates *judgment* —Judgment activates *Shame* —Shame activates *Anger* —Unchecked Anger activates *Rage* —Rage activates *mental illness,* especially for the mentally ill without good coping skills. Rejection ultimately leads *isolation* and more *delusions.*

When you are swamped and overwhelmed by life, how do you avoid falling into bad habits and avoidance behavior? What self-talk or thoughts do you use to push forward despite the significant challenges?

"Sometimes when you're overwhelmed by a situation - when you're in the darkest of darkness - that's when your priorities are reordered"—Phoebe Snow

When I am overwhelmed by life, I have to first and foremost take care of my mental health. If I don't have my mental health, every other aspect of my life, whether it be meaningful relationships or taking care of priorities in life; they all suffer. Frankly speaking my Heaven on Earth lies in my mind and I need to take care of it. Health of the mind is the most important thing to me. If I don't have that, I don't have anything, anyway. I can not stress that enough. That's why I will repeat that statement once again in order to emphasize it.

Health of the mind is the most important thing to me. If I don't have that, I don't have anything, anyway.
I lost my health once and today I treasure it beyond the measure of material possessions. Health is wealth to me. I invest a lot of time, effort and work in doing things to get better in dealing with difficult challenges

and overwhelming struggles. Living used to be a big challenge but today I have progressive victory over my challenges.

Now, that does not mean that I am immune to difficulties. On a contrary. I recognize that I can easily get overwhelmed if I let it, so I counter that by sharpening the saw often, along and using my tools to stay on top of things before they grow to epic proportions. I dig out the weeds before they get too difficult to handle and they obstruct a healthy garden- my life.

As a sensitive individual, I have to do self-care and stay on top of it, lest I fall prey to detrimental activities as my past life clearly reflects. It used to be a mess of my own creation. Moreover, I don't shut the door on my past. I remember it and use my memory bank to avoid pitfalls common to my psyche and learn from repeated mistakes, eventually.

I accept how I feel. Feelings are the most important thing in life. People may not know but everything in life, the good and the bad arises from feelings and emotions. People are wired throughout the body to feel and experience sensations. In the past, I always judged my feelings as something that I should not feel. That in itself caused much suffering because on top of feelings, my thought processes would not allow me to properly experience them. I would mask them and self medicate or entertain more overwhelming thoughts that brought even more destructive emotions. I would self-combust emotionally.

Today I am on fire from time to time but it's a different type fire. Today I see joy in most of my days. Today I also accept my feelings. They are my feelings and it's quite okay to feel and experience them. I try to express them in a healthy manner if I'm mindful enough. I talk about how I feel and I connect with people. I am allowed to express how I feel. I can say that I feel anxious, angry sad or whatever the case may be. I journal how I feel and magic happens. I dig deep and try to understand what is going on with my life. I do things that I enjoy doing. I have few hobbies that I like to do and when I do them, I am in the present moment. Being in the present moment means I am enjoying the moment and I'm living in it without dwelling on the past or the future.

I don't tackle my whole life problem all at once. I take it piece-meal. I live through this day only. Yesterday or tomorrow rarely matter to me. I have learned that the past and the future are illusions. They don't exist. The moment I realized that, most of my pain and suffering went away. This outlook cured my depression. I am free of it if I do maintenance on my mental health. I do short repetitive prayers to the chief of staff upstairs if I obsess over something that happened. I focus my thoughts on God as I understand the Creator—Today it's Jesus Christ.

I do some self-care. Calming music, hot bath, good meal, TV show. I ask people in my life for advice on my overwhelming situation. I have to remember that my overwhelming emotions can cause me to activate a built-in forgetter. I need to be reminded what to do sometimes because the head can play tricks on my mind.

Acceptance is the key, as is change. I change me and I already have changed the world. I help someone else change and now I have changed the world two times over. Sometimes I myself need help. I try to be available to others. When I do that, I forget about my own little problems. I have a great support system and people in my life. I am very fortunate individual.

I run on the highest octane fuel in the universe called gratitude. From attitude to gratitude to yes I can attitude. Yes. I can and I will overcome my challenges. I laugh at some of that stuff too. Laughter is best medicine. I think positive and positive things happen in my life. I say or think things like:

"This too shall pass"

"Easy does it but do it"

I have to accept it. Acceptance is the key but I need to keep working on changing things for the better. *"God grant me serenity to accept the things I cannot change. Courage to change the things I can. And the wisdom to know the difference."*

At least I am alive. I could be dead and nothing would matter. I get to experience the good and the bad. I am grateful to be alive, I really am. As long as I am alive, I still have a chance. Some people have it much worse but they get through it. I will too. Gratitude is my default mode. Life is extremely precious and should not be squandered.

Who has gone from a normal situation to a catastrophic personal situation in less than 1 hour?

"Once you choose hope, anything's possible"—Christopher Reeve

The above quote is in a wrong context here, but hope is a key to life. However, how about this lady I read about without mentioning her name in Hope Mills, N. C. An airplane crashed into her house and killed her husband, and injured her, half an hour before midnight.

Just when you're hoping to get some rest and think you're safely tucked in the comfort of your blanket. You're readying yourself for sleep in the safely of own home, thinking about the next day and what it will bring when the unforeseen disaster strikes. Therefore, it's important to run on the highest octane fuel in the Universe—gratitude as opposed to an attitude and count ones blessings instead of bruises.

Who would you like to see sober?

"Getting sober was one of the three pivotal events in my life, along with becoming an actor and having a child. Of the three, finding my sobriety was the hardest thing"—Gary Oldman

If I could have one wish in the world, I'd wish —given a wish from a genie in the bottle—that anyone who struggles with addiction no longer did so. Alcoholism and addiction is a very debilitating and lonely illness as it is misunderstood. There comes a point, even those in rich social life are an isolated bunch in the company of many—things rarely get better without help.

Addiction is a disease of compulsion, feelings and emotions that sometimes come and go as they please, giving a false sense of recovery but in reality, People stop getting better. It's the only disease that convinces sufferers they have no disease and that they can handle one more with impunity. And the person I would like most to get sober, I do not wish to speak publicly about.

How were you able to overcome a difficult life experience?

"In the middle of every difficulty lies

opportunity"—Albert Einstein

Years of therapy, recovery mindset, abstinence from mind-altering substances and toxic people, all a continuous process. Positive influences as well. Never ends, but gets better over time as the process continues. Not every day is a pink cloud, but much more of those than dark clouds.

Basically a lot of my obsessions and compulsions, addictions and delusions, I direct into recovery and improvement in some ways, in a nut shell. And I overcame difficult experience by surviving it and not dying. As I go through the feelings and situations, I learn to cope with it better on some days as opposed to others. Recovery is not linear but with ups and downs. It has its own roller-coaster and seasons too.

What do you think of when you read or hear "to make something out of nothing"?

"Learning is a result of listening, which in turn leads to even better listening and attentiveness to the other person. In other words, to learn from the child, we must have empathy, and empathy grows as we learn"–Alice Miller

I think that whoever says that to someone else ought to rethink saying it. Obviously it's something if it bothers another. One of the worst things between interaction of one person with another is not to acknowledge other people's feelings or concerns because dismissing it has bigger implications in the future. It leads to isolation, addiction and a person learns to dismiss their own concerns as invalid.

My problem to you may be trivial but to me it could be a big deal and if I can't come to you with it, another time I may dismiss it as well. Or learn that I make something out of nothing and then I begin to internalize my feelings without properly expressing them.

The nature of the feelings is such that sooner or later they have to go somewhere. Especially with men, it is often thought and taught not to talk about stuff and learn to deal with it.
"Men don't cry"
We know how that goes when everything is internalized and the pressure not consistently released.

What is an impossible thing you've thought of today?

"A person who thinks all the time has nothing to think about except thoughts. So, he loses touch with reality, and lives in a world of illusions"—Alan Watts

I thought how wonderful it would be to stop thinking, was what I was thinking about, and instead focusing on nothing—perhaps breathe only and let my mind rest. That was what I thought about today and it felt impossible for the time being—more practice needed.

How do you stop feeling scared because you're falling behind in life compared to your peers?

"Don't compare yourself with other people; compare yourself with who you were yesterday"—Jordan Peterson

I'm not scared by falling beyond but I once was and I compared myself to others. I didn't fall behind, I fell to the bottom of the barrel and now there is nowhere to go but up.

Today I'm living my own life and no one else's. Not theirs. If one has to get rid of Face Book and all that stuff in order not to compare one's life to theirs or any distraction that doesn't move one forward, then that needs to happen. If a person keeps busy improving their own life, they don't have time to feel scared of others leaving them behind. Others are scared because they can't see you anymore. And not because you're behind, but because you're in the front, waiting and waiving with a nice surprise . . . Light that fire and roll with a positive mindset. Lead the way with a torch and a maverick's mindset.

How can an individual psychologically overcome pride?

"Pride must die in you, or nothing of heaven can live in you"—Andrew Murray

Pride is good in its proper balance. It is the feeling of worthiness and confidence. Being proud of ones's abilities and a family roots for example, enables an individual to function in a world like a normal human being. If the pride doesn't boast or become stubborn and closed minded, it has a place in society as people should perform tasks and job with pride and conviction. It increases self-esteem and allows fulfilment of goals. It can also be the last thing standing before a humiliating fall and pride is the sin the begets all others.

An individual overcomes pride with humility. The only way I can think of an individual's psychologically overcoming pride, is through an ego deflation. Ego runs the mind with its own willfulness. An individual diminishes self importance, selfishness and self-seeking motives. Realizing a person's sinful nature and confession with another opens up vulnerability. By admitting faults and wrong doings such action humiliates and humbles a person. Now someone knows you secrets. Asking God to remove shortcomings and defects of character, by first being aware of them and then humbly asking God to remove them. Being humble and grateful overcomes pride. I don't believe a person can truly do that on their own, if people are only relying on themselves and the material world. They have to their pride and behavior is wrong. Repentance and renunciation of old ways has to happen.

"God is dead"

Nietzsche used the phrase to express his idea that the Enlightenment had eliminated the possibility of the existence of God. And so, more and more people, exactly with that attitude became their own gods and pride flourished ever more. People no longer needed God, so there is no need to look towards higher ideas and change. Even for people that do believe in God, that's not always enough. Pride leads to suffering because someone always wants to get something; control something and when it doesn't happen more friction follows.

CHAPTER VII - MORALITY-VIRTUES - PRINCIPLES

What does it mean to organize life with integrity?

"Moral authority comes from following universal and timeless principles like honesty, integrity, treating people with respect"—Stephen Covey

Organizing life with integrity means to focus on principles and virtues and build life around them. One example would be to incorporate moral, philosophical or religious world view such as that of Christian tenets and principles focused on action of compassion, humility, gratitude, patience, charity, honesty, kindness, moderation for example. Integrity is an umbrella term higher concept that allows individuals not to fall into the trap of materialism, vanity, superficiality, overindulgence, lust after people and things, and compulsions for abuse. Progressive victory over those things I suppose matter more, since we're talking organizing one's life with integrity and progress rather than perfection is more attainable, although less desirable in the long term. With practice, I believe integrity means to perfect oneself morally, principally and spiritually as God would have us represent His nature.

When a person who doesn't have any conscious at all does something immoral, can he or she keep going on with it without any hesitation between time to time, without at least making some self-justification, why or why not?

"Everything I like is either illegal, immoral or fattening"—Alexander Woollcott

If the question you ask has to do with someone you know, here is what I believe may be happening. You might be dealing with a gold digger, shallow individual, narcissist, sociopath or straight up psychopath who doesn't care about anything but themselves and their conscious drives reflect their behavior. Morality is irrelevant when it comes to their behavior because such individuals lack it or suppress it to the point of no return at the time of engagement. There is no rhyme or reason because some people just don't operate in societal parameters.

You know how she or he is . . . stay away . . . even if the sex is great, if that is what's holding someone to that person. Sex can be used as a powerful weapon of control and manipulation without remorse, shame or regret on the part of the manipulator. Victims come back like a lamb to a slaughter-house instead of steering clear of dangerous influence.

Every time someone like that does something immoral they don't have to keep justifying their reasoning or excuse for that action. They have justified it enough and now it's an automatic behavior. They do something because it benefits them in some way. They rather win and you lose than mutually benefit. They keep going until they are found out or stopped. When they are found out, they usually go to the next victim until the law catches up to them, which in most cases it does. Habitual immorality makes these individuals more brazen and bolder and they up their game to the new levels and heights.

CHAPTER VIII - NATURE OF REALITY

How do I disprove a fear of not being in the real world?

"This critique also misreads the Copernican revolution. Yes, our perceptions misled us about our place in the universe. But its deeper message is this: our perceptions can mislead us about the very nature of the universe itself. We are prone to false believe that certain limitations and idiosyncrasies of our perceptions are genuine insights into objective reality"—Donald D. Hoffman

Let's face it. Living in reality can be a scary proposition. But what is reality really? Reality is how people perceive the world around them, and for one person to the next, reality may differ quite a bit. Subjective lenses of the person experiencing conscious reality may be a difference between living in fear and living unobstructed by a fear inducing mental construct, for example.

There is a lot that can be said about the nature of reality. Most people could come to the consensus that reality — objective and visual — is almost the same for everyone in regard to the material world and the five senses it invokes, but is it really? We could be wired to experience reality one way, when indeed peoples' brains reconstruct the world as they need it, not as it really is, like a virtual reality headset that someone puts on. According to the scientific evidence, reality may be quite different than what people experience.

According to Donald Hoffman, a cognitive psychologist, we live in a simulation. An example could be an interface, like a file icon on the computer.When you press that file and open it, does it mean it's exactly there or looks exactly how it's seen? No. It's a short cut redirecting that file from inside the electronic components of the computer circuits, chips and transistors. And also upon a closer inspection, the screen reveals multitude of pixels that make the entirety of the screen. Hence reality, could have similar tendencies and collective human brains process and see what they need to, in order to survive and thrive on the planet Earth. That's one possibility.

Another possibility is that on the same plan of our reality and the material world is another dimension altogether, occupying the same space — let's call it a spiritual realm. We know that's the case because the bible speaks about the spirit world and dark principalities that influence humanity. Nevertheless, If someone has a fear of not being in a real world, it's important to talk about it with someone and practice anxiety countering techniques to overcome those and any other fears that come up. The key is to accept things as they stand and change how one feels about things. It's a fact this question was asked and answered. That's real. It's a fact that people feel, and especially feel fearful emotions, although those fears may not be facts for other people. After all, fears are intangible beliefs, product of mental constructs as well as past experiences. They ought to be addressed to increase the quality of one's life if it's a persistent issue.

How much are you in control of your own perception?

"The only thing that really matters now is whether man can climb up to a higher moral level, to a higher plane of consciousness, in order to be equal to the superhuman powers which the fallen angels have played into his hands. But he can make no progress until he becomes very much better acquainted with his own nature"—Carl Jung

I always control my perception if it's my perception to a degree, but equally well everyday. However, whether that perception is real is another story. Perhaps, it's my perception of the world that controls my thoughts and action. I have a great deal of control afterwards, after the given situation, but not always at the moment of life showing up. I have enough control to self-reflect and realize where I went wrong on a grand perspective. Some people may not even think anything wrong occurred in the interaction, but I will, because there are issues I'd like get better with, and I have a standard — a measuring stick to measure my perception with. So that's that. A case in point may be my filter or boundaries with others.

In relation to issues that include politics, policy or world affairs, I also have a standard of measurement and enough of history lessons to predict which way things are unfolding or where we are heading into the future, without the need to rely on a crystal ball — sources of info I use to support my perceptions, although how that info makes me feel skews my perception for the moment (If it makes sense what I'm writing here…basically feelings and emotions get in the way that shifts my perception and not the perception itself like the fact that things are heading from bad to worse.

Would it be wrong if I had that perception in light of world developments? I may have a bad reaction to what I hear or learn for the day. Hence, sometimes it's just better not to know or know without knowing and focus on the control I have here and now, without imposing it on someone else.

My other perception is that control is an illusion. No one has control. People may think or feel like they're in control until that person learns that it isn't so. It's silly to think that one is fully in charge, unless that person or people have a God complex— a definite delusion. So it happens that people in global positions of power are in fact delusional. That's my perception and observation thus far, even if idolized by majority, because 51 percent doesn't by default make it right. Majority is/are? often wrong. I wish I could tell them personally and burst their bubbles, but I suspect they have swallowed the (cool)aid long ago, as I have in my own way. And it wouldn't do any good anyway. You can't fix it with your own thinking. That's what got us in trouble in the first place. The hard drive is already corrupted.

CHAPTER IX - PERSONAL QUESTIONS

Who are you today?

*"Reach for the stars, and if you end
up on the moon, that's good too.
Wolves howl. I write"*—GTStarr

Just another person among billions of special or potentially special people like stars in the unlit night skies. I try to learn to accept myself and the world and spread the feeling as best as I possibly can, which is something I do better now than before. I'm a person who's getting in touch with himself to find out what lies underneath.

Who's chasing you down?

"The happiness of your life depends upon the quality of your thoughts"—Marcus Aurelius

My mortality is chasing me down. I'm not as resilient, sharp and strong as I used to be. The decline and entropy is inevitable in all temporal life forces. Maybe I never was the fullest copybook at school, but I filled in the pages and winged it as best as I knew how, when inspection came around. The demons of the past also surface from time to time and try to sabotage my life. To add to the challenge, everyday frustrations seek my downfall and so patience and tolerance is a must in order to overcome those feelings.

How far do your thoughts randomly wander?

"Listen to your hunches, pay attention to your intuition, do not dismiss your random thoughts, inspirations or ideas.... They could be giving you the best advice you ever had..."— Neale Donald Walsch

Randomly my thoughts go to conversations I had in the past weeks and I actually have out loud conversations with the person I was speaking with without even knowing until my wife asked:

"Who are You talking to?"

"Oh, just a colleague from work,"

And we both laugh. Then I think to myself:
Dude, you're nuts. You better get a grip on yourself.

I question the execution of my conversations and sometimes I wonder if I said the right things. I can be my own best friend and my own worst enemy from time to time. I am working on proper boundaries. In truth however, I'm getting much better with things and life got much more bearable since I became sober and in recovery. Sometimes though, I "can" be very self-critical and judgmental of myself and the mistakes I make, especially when I self-reflect on my life and seek to understand my thought processes.

I have done a lot of inappropriate humor in life and then I question myself: Why are my boundaries so mess up?

But then I think . . . You only drank or got high for close to 30 years of your life. You're emotionally a bit stunted so give it some time. In deed I'm getting better with that, but here it is. My joke. No one is allowed to take a credit for this one: LOL

"How many alcoholics does it take to drink a case of beer?"

"How many?"

"Two."

"Dr. Jekyll and Mr. Hyde."

If You don't get it, don't worry. You're probably not an alcoholic. Lol.

What is your "I lived through that" event?

"The ultimate value of life depends upon awareness and the power of contemplation rather than upon mere survival"—Aristotle

Survival expert so far LOL. Lived through three accidental near drowning. Lived through four accidental overdoses. A few alcohol blackouts. Got hit by a car once—landed on my head. Fell off a house roof once too and a high fence, landing next to a huge concrete block—hard landing anyway— took my breath away for a while and I thought I'm going to suffocate without air.

Been through major depression—doom and gloom; survived that. Suffered anxiety—self medicated all my life. Traumatic experiences in life too. Ethnic neighborhood discrimination and violence. Many fist fights. Multiple medical and physical trauma emergencies. Abandonment issues. Not always being a victim—was at fault too. Hopelessness, fear, doubt and uncertainty.

Panic attacks that I thought are going to kill me. Delusions, "situational" paranoia.

Anger and rage issues have been part of my life as well. Thirty years of treated and untreated alcoholism, addiction and social anxiety unless under the influence. Jails and institutions—not fun. Numerous other losses. Lived to be able to write a fiction novel, although could have just wrote about life.

Today I celebrate 3 years of unconditional sobriety —June 21st—first day of summer—new beginning through my Higher Power—been at it for 20 + years trying to get it, persisted and won one day at a time. God got me through it and the power of healing through 12 Step Programs, guidance of a Sponsor and people in recovery in general. I would be the biggest fool not to see it that way . . . TODAY-To Thine Own Self Be True. Unity—Service—Recovery

What is the most embarrassing situation that you have woken up to?

"When I was a little kid, I used to really embarrass my parents"—Russell Crowe

One of my most embarrassing moments (there were a few naturally) was drinking a liter of vodka by myself the night before. Next day I was replaying what transpired. The pieces of a puzzle were missing from the black out and brain damage that I sustained that wonderful evening of my own creation.

It was a New Year's festivity and my then employers invited me to celebrate along with them and their families to a nice restaurant with live entertainment. Boy, did I show my true colors. And I wasn't shining either.Maybe I was thinking I was drinking a lemonade. Either way, I came to a startling conclusion. I had a problem with alcohol. My boss had to drive me home. I could not give him coherent directions since obviously I was checked out and the trip home was slightly extended to put it lightly. He caught a flat tire from my understanding or some other issue I am no longer able to recall. Until today I have no clear clue what happened. When Ed told me some of the things that took place at the event and on the way home, my selective hearing kicked in in to order not to relive the horror movie that would unfold in my head. I spent the next three days in bed curing a horrible hang over, shaking from alcohol poisoning and replaying the disaster- namely my life. I was in my early twenties then.

I was burning with shame. I promised myself I will mend my ways and do better. I didn't. The promises were empty words or thoughts to make myself feel better while I ran on fear and embarrassment. They were empty and vain as was I. There was little essence and substance in my life. More embarrassments, shame, pain and sufferings followed in years to come. Some people need to hit all the bottoms there are in life in order to learn. That is of course if they come out alive. One can not blame anyone but themselves if they stumble twice over the same rock. I stumbled over it to the point I lost count.

I always took my will back. My bottoms had more bottoms, but I survived and they made me the person I am today. I'm still healing the clouded judgment. Lots of experience. Fewer brain cells but alive. Addiction had a grip on me and my life. Along with me, family and friends suffered. That was then.

Today, don't shut the door on my past. I use my past to help myself and others. Pain was mandatory but suffering was up to me. It was always up to me. I didn't know any better or ignorance took a driver seat. In this example, ignorance of my illness was in the back seat unresponsive for most or at least part of the journey home and throughout life.

If anyone is struggling with addiction, please get help. Recovery is possible. It will happen when we genuinely seek help, accept ourselves for who we are and change. It's a contradiction in the same sentence. Human nature is full of contradictions. It's called life but I have to be honest about my dishonesty because I can rationalize and explain everything away in my life. It will happen when people genuinely seek help, *"accept"* oneself for who they area work on *"change."* If we don't change our sobriety date will change if we live to see it! Fear = Face Everything and Recover (not fear everything and run)

CHAPTER X - PHILOSOPHY AND GOD

**When conclusions are made about life,
is that freeing or restrictive?**

Stand fast therefore in the liberty wherewith Christ hath made us free, and be not entangled again with the yoke of bondage—Galatians 5:1 (KJV)

I belive there is more freedom and peace in God because the world makes us chase the worldy things, and we lose ourselves doing that. My conclusion is that without God, people become their own gods. So it's both initially. Lots of freedom leads to depravity and lust to covet over people and things and live life without other restrictions. It feels like freedom, but it's actually a worldly bondage and dependance. It is suffering in its later stages as life and expectations bring about much disappointment and suffering. Dependence on God curbs instincts and neuroticism, which actually happen to be a norm today, bordering on mass psychosis. Dependence on God defines boundaries and feels restrictive, but enables independence from the world—true happiness and connection to God and the worldly creatures. It's not a false but a genuine filler. Therefore dependence on God, is in fact independence and freedom from bondage of the world . . . coming from a person addicted to everything.

What do you think of the phrase "Never underestimate yourself and never overestimate others"

"Never underestimate your power to change yourself"—H. Jackson Brown, Jr.

When people don't compete with each other, they don't have to worry about all that. We're one family on a larger cosmic scale thriving when cooperating with one another. People are very capable creatures when they tap into their potential but often sell themselves short when they look at others.

Therefore, one ought to compare oneself to oneself from one day to the next. Because of my belief in consciousness outside the mind, what we really shouldn't underestimate are evil principalities that implant dark thoughts and make people fight and fear one another, and live in sin. I believe they're real and live outside our dimension.

When most people you grew up with have died, is there anything worth living for?

"Peace I leave with you, my peace I give unto you: not as the world giveth, give I unto you. Let not your heart be troubled, neither let it be afraid"—John 14:27 (KJV)

I would have to say most definitely. Life goes on. However long is left for us, we have to keep going because the best is yet to come is my belief. I don't believe this life is all there is while in this plain of existence. One ought to strive for the ultimate connection with force living in all dimensions, The God of the Universe and His so Jesus Christ. I firmly believe reality as is experienced is not what really exists and blinds people to the ultimate truth. That's why consciousness exists outside of our minds. I'm more than certain of that.

Our wiring and senses can not detect all that is. For all we know, those that passed away really did not. They crossed over to the other side. They have crossed over to the other plain and dimension and while not here, they still exist. They went to one of the two places the bible speaks about and those are heaven or hell. I believe people need to repent of their sins and ways and call onto Jesus Christ, our Lord and savior to be saved.

There is no death. Spiritual death does not exist but there is such a thing as the second death. That's the seperation from God's love and isolation in the everlasting lake of fire.

I used to believe there is only transition or journey home as is so prevalent in the new age movement. If we don't pass the test, we have to repeat the class. We repeat the class by being reincarnated until the mission is complete and the soul returns home to God...purest light and joy. Well, that's what the reincarnation teachers and people propagate. I used to be on that band wagon, however I think that while on Earth, we have one chance to get it right and we end up in heaven or hell, because if God exists, Satan must also be real and He is deceptive with all that New Age lie to make people thing everything will be okay. If you don't get it this lifetime, you'll get plenty of chance. The point of life is to live first and foremost for the glory of God through his love and grace and through faith.

95

CHAPTER XI - PSYCHOLOGY
OF THE MIND

How dangerous is it to let people define themselves?

"Defining yourself through thought is limiting yourself"—Eckhart Tolle

When people define themselves, they might as put themselves in a box and label themselves. Perhaps even ship themselves into control of someone or something else. Because if someone defines themselves, they may whole heartedly believe they will never get better or overcome some challenge, underlying condition, diagnosis and there is nothing they can do about it. It's basically a perpetual self-sabotage. That's in contrast with someone who identifies with something for the purpose of obtaining awareness, acceptance, the healing tools snd working on a given issue—change.

Why do some people gravitate to fear in the face of disaster, more so than seeking an optimistic solution or hope?

"The child is a father of the man"—
William Wordsworth

It all stems from childhood I believe. If a child had not learned good coping and thinking skills or was neglected in some way with fear exacerbated, they will naturally tend to look on a negative side of things. That outlook is ingrained and further controls future thinking because fear had been prevalent in their life from a start. In adulthood these children run a childhood program—aka Matrix.

Whenever I face danger or think that I am facing a life-threatening situation I try to immediately turn to my "real" me, try to become self-conscious and "aware" of that moment. I think that by doing that I will survive it. Why is that?

"God wants us to know we are saved, for saved people are dangerous people, willing to face off with the world, unafraid of the consequences since they know that, whatever happens, they will have eternal life"—Max Lucado

When you get out of the head and experience the moment you are more vigilant and aware of the surroundings and yourself. You experience life as it should be experienced without projecting later events or reevaluating past actions. Action happens now in the moment where abstract thinking is secondary and concrete awareness presides. Everything else in the head is either driven by created ego, fear, insecurities, and learned automatic responses of self through acquisition of lifelong experiences and interactions between other people and learned behavior.

Being in a moment counters fear which can paralyze a person or cause mental retrogression due to fear of life-threatening event or incoming trauma. Not so when in the present moment. But it costs. One has to pay attention to the moment and that may be very hard to attain during difficulties and trials.

What psychological tricks work on most people?

"The pendulum of the mind oscillates between sense and nonsense, not between right and wrong"—Carl Gustav Jung

I told a guy once that he is looking very sharp in that suit. Next thing you know he's looking in a mirror in another part of the establishment believing it and feeling good about his own inadequacies. He wasn't a big fan of mine. Sometimes you just have to soften them up and validate them, but not in a mean spirited, manipulate way. In a loving and gentle way. Everyone needs a self-esteem boots from time to time.

**What's the best mindset to help
conquer a fear of taking risks?**

"Nothing in life is worthwhile unless you

take risks"—Denzel Washington

To realize one is alive is to be aware of potential possibilities and risks. "Still alive, still have a chance," I often say. "It could be worse, we could be dead". What's the worst that can happen for the one that knows death is not all? God could and God would if God was sought. Ask God every day for help and take some risks if you feel like it calls you without the greater urge to destroy your life.

What can't I get if I'm not as good as you?

"It is better to conquer yourself than to win a thousand battles. Then the victory is yours. It cannot be taken from you, not by angels or by demons, heaven or hell"—Buddha

I'm not sure how to respond to this question. I don't think I'm better or worse than anyone else. I think we all could improve with things and life in general and learn something from the next person and never look down at people. When I start finding faults with people, I really need to take a look at myself because the problem lies within. You're okay the way you are unless you decide you're not. I only compare myself to myself from one day to the next; this I see is the best outlook on compensation with others. You can get whatever you put your mind to up to a reasonable limit.

What is a personality disorder?

"I don't think people understand how stressful it is to explain what's going on in your head when you don't even understand it yourself"—Sara Quin

Personality Disorder is inner conflict within a person that affects feelings, behaviors and healthy thought processes. It is maladjustment and a source of significant issues for the person experiencing these disruptions of normal functioning. I would like to best describe them as internal battles or outright war within. Personality disruption affects how individuals view themselves and the world around them. When left unchecked or untreated, it inevitably impact others by mere proximity and even if treated things won't be perfect. Personality disorders are only confirmed in adulthood since children do not have developed solid personality or are still shaped by outside factors. An exception may be Antisocial Personality Disorder. These disorders create enormous clash and instability within adults who qualify for a particular diagnosis.

Personality disorders are out of balance coping mechanism as I come to understand them through my own past maladaptive ways of dealing with life. They begin early in childhood and as such spiral out of control as the person becomes of age. They may be persistent or have peaking onsets depending on the levels of stresses involved. There can be a multifaceted number of reasons as to why they occur and various issues that were/are present. It is safe to say that in the majority of cases, there exists a trigger or multitude of initiating protagonists.

Often family disruption, dysfunction or both is present. A trauma may or may not be involved, experienced or other set of distressing events taken place. Children may have been neglected emotionally/physically/sexually. The resulting coping mechanisms are distressful feelings and emotions turned inward or projected outward through abnormal behaviors in order to gain attention, validation and acceptance. Sometimes children may want to impress others to feel connected. At other times, they may want to hurt others. Also, during distressful events or circumstances, thoughts are entertained that can further add to the distortion of reality or enable a person to escape into fantasy as a method of protecting the mind from further trauma or distress.

Important to note is that a small percentage of children are likely sensitive to their surroundings and therefore various experiences can influence these individuals more severely than general population. While in great measure it is certainly genetic, upbringing plays a huge role in later development and intensity of symptoms. The brain chemistry and neural wiring is altered as well. Therefore, it is a combination of nature and nurture. Initially, the coping mechanism serves a purpose until it outstays its welcome and creates more challenges than it was initially intended to relieve. Self-medication through addictive behaviors or substances can also result periodically. That will probably compound severity of symptoms or will exacerbate them altogether. Attempted suicides, successful suicides or accidental overdoses are greater in those qualified for personality disorders.

There are three main personality disorder clusters.

Cluster A personality disorders

Cluster A personality disorders are characterized by peculiar, being eccentric, without of the normal thinking or behavior. These are:

Paranoid personality disorder

Schizoid personality disorder

Schizotypal personality disorder

Cluster B personality disorder

Cluster B personality disorders are characterized by more dramatic, difficult to control emotions, unstable thinking and/or behaviors. I am mostly familiar with this cluster.

Antisocial personality disorder/Sociopathy

Borderline personality disorder/ chameleon taking on its environment

Histrionic personality disorder

Narcissistic personality disorder/ego maniac with inferiority complex

Cluster C personality disorders

Cluster C personality disorders are characterized by anxious, fearful thought processes or behavior.

Avoidant personality disorder

Dependent personality disorder

Obsessive-compulsive personality disorder.

(Mayo clinic online reference)

Many of these personality disorders are interchangeable and an individual may exhibit overlap of symptoms that spills from one disorder to another. There has to be a number of symptoms present in order to qualify for anyone disorder. In truth, many people who do not qualify for rigid diagnosis may also be suffering any number of symptoms during periods of intense stress or unfavorable events or their own distorted coping mechanisms. It is very easy to label or mislabel someone.

On a good note now. *Personality disorders * are disorders that can be worked on if individuals understand that issues are present and change is sought after. Therefore, personality disorder can, to a large degree be overcome or at least maintained through self-awareness. If there is a problem, there is a solution. If no problem exists, the solution does not either. Self-awareness is key and coupled with consistent, persistent treatment and recovery, some individuals may within time no longer qualify for the disorder itself.

I do not claim to be an expert on personality disorders. I share my experiences, thoughts and a bit of my research on the matter.

What are the recovery rates of people who suffer with BPD?

"My skin is so thin that the innocent words of others burn holes right through me" —Unknown

According to the research The lived experience of recovery in borderline personality disorder: a qualitative study by Fiona Y. Y. Michelle L. Townsend, Caitlin E. Miller, Mahlie Jewell and Brin F. S. Grenyer from 2019, the recovery ranges from 33 to 99%. A total of 171 individuals provided contact details for follow-up from the online survey, where 108

individuals were contacted. Thirty-nine individuals completed the
telephone interview. Using the study's inclusion criteria,
14 individual narratives (7 recovered and 7 not recovered) were included in the study. All individuals in this study were female with an average age of 33.36 years. Recovery in borderline personality disorder (BPD) occurred across three main stages, including; 1) being stuck, 2) diagnosis, and 3) improving.

My personal belief is that most people with the disorder are able to recover. Many people get better with time and the severity of the onsets tends to lessen as they understand what's going on with them and arm themselves with proper knowledge and tools and work the recovery process. The best outcome would be that an individual fully integrates their sense of self as one psychologist or doctor put it, and therefore fully recover. Only an individual stops her or his healing.

The recovery rate for people with BPD is 100 percent if recovery is number one priority in life. A lot has to do with proper motivation and pride that stands in the way, along with rationalizing the illness. Borderline Personality Disorder is not a cognitive disorder in which a person is unable to overcome struggles and challenges but one that deals with unregulated emotions accompanied with distorted thought processes that cause severe emotional distress. Although it's a serious disorder, it can be overcome with adequate plan and action. Individuals with this disorder need to take their recovery seriously if they truly desire lasting results. I know many people are serious and try but I'm talking solid commitment, therapy, workbooks and all the tools possible and available. It isn't easy and I'll be the first one to admit that, but quitting is not an option. Not at all. It's a mission for sure.

Naturally. overwhelming emotions will take place, however they will take place less and less and eventually extreme reactions diminish to that of a regular person if all the warning signs are taken into account and the work is being done. People have emotional relapses and that too is part of the process and growth.

If someone's primary goal in life is a millionaire status, they will, no matter what that entails. Whether the venture will survive or fall flat on its face is a different question and answer. If someone who struggles with BPD is aware and knows what is going on with them, then one can absolutely overcome it and be successful in life. Occasional struggle can be like that of any person. Sufferers have to know how they operate and what triggers the onset of overwhelming emotions. It's a quest of self-discovery and learning adequate coping skills and behavioral modification. Acceptance of the condition and willingness to change is crucial in order to recover.

Where does selfishness come from? Do babies start out equal in terms of 'self-focus' and how do life experiences change that over time? Why does one person look excessively inward to satisfying their own wants while others seek empathetic service?

"Almost every sinful action ever committed can be traced back to a selfish motive. It is a trait we hate in other people but justify in ourselves—Stephen Kendrick

There are a variety of takes this answer can be focused on and many ways to tackle it. I will focus on a partial aspect without diving too deep. Today I watched a very interesting, informative show about the human brain and I'm coming from that perspective only.

If we're to assume (that's all we can do) that evolution is true, then it would make sense that first and foremost, people (some more than others) on many levels use the primitive, reptilian brain quite more frequently but unnecessarily under normal circumstances—designed for extreme survival under duress—which in civilized society can be misleading and misused. However, from the creation point of view that makes sense as well. One can also claim, that a God given instinct are, well . . . God given and natural. But as with anything, even instincts are abused and misused for self-serving benefits. People are naturally self-oriented towards individual and family survival with obvious degrees but especially without the established principles such as the golden rule for instance:

> *The Golden Rule is the principle of treating others as one wants to be treated. Various expressions of this rule can be found in the tenets of most religions and creeds through the ages. It can be considered an ethic of reciprocity in some religions, although different religions treat it differently-* Wikipedia

One of the active and relevant brain parts in regards to selfishness is amygdala. Amygdala serves as a switch whereby regulating multitude of functions and emotions. It's like a relay between lower and higher brain functions. Fear, aggression and primitive drives are responsible for competition with the world. Competition thus, lowers the function of the higher brain. Frontal lobe is responsible for expression of higher ideas, cooperation, planning and pleasurable feelings that come with empathy and compassion. Some people use that part of the brain more frequently which may indicate they have developed more as a collective human species.

However, different cultures, reinforce competition and primitive drives, as in sports such as football. Although it is a team effort, it's primal and aggressive. Individuals are encouraged to embrace roughness and winning. In a sense, selfishness drives human success but often at the expense of others. Some children thrive more on aggressive sports, while others choose activities enhancing artistic expression and promoting creativity. That does not mean it's always that way, but the more active the children are, they're likely more aggressive and generally more outgoing, which could stimulate the amygdala further and increase primitive brain further. Primitive drives are awakened and entertained more frequently with aggressive children and with raging hormones, they may not think clearly (most kids don't reason well without supervision) and rationally and are likely to get in trouble through selfish and self oriented goals. It makes perfect sense—selfishness is encouraged and rewarded. Lots of value is, was and will be placed on physical prowess. This had a place in all societies throughout the history. The more competition emphasized—the more aggression and less empathy naturally.

And again competition. No need to look further than sports in America. Players are treated like gods and violent, competitive sports are adored. It is how it is. We do live in modern Rome, and people seek that entertainment and stimulation that opens up those drives people crave. American football, MMA, boxing, WWE are all violent. It's not a rule that these sports promote selfishness but rather people place more emphasis on them than personal growth, which promotes empathy and compassion.

In short, if the amygdala is on full blast, the other part of the higher brain are diminished. This makes lots of sense to me because both area of the brain cannot be equally activated. One supersedes the other. I think individualistic societies on the go promote the activation of lower brain more frequently again, through competition in school, grade system and the likes, which for the competitive society driven to succeed makes perfect sense. This may hurt some children who are forced to study things they have little interest in and thus kill the creative and empathetic side, while increasing the aggressive brain responsible for rage, jealousy, hedonism, violence, conquest, dominion over others and being the best at something or trying too hard. This is an assumption also, and a simplistic way of looking at things, but perhaps it's a little piece of a greater puzzle.

Moreover, even in academia, the system and some parents encourage strong competition as a default outlook, because if one wants to enter the best college for example, they need to compete with others who want to get there too. More stress, more anxiety, more performance, more focus on me, means less focus on you. When one stresses, one regresses. Selfishness is a learned behavior as well.

How does owning your own mistakes help to build character and mental strength?

"Mistakes are always forgivable if one has the courage to admit them"—Bruce Lee

Owning my own mistakes is humiliating and shaming—a humbling experience. If I told you my mistakes, flaws and my defects that wouldn't increase my pride. It would lower my pride. I don't want to tell you my vulnerabilities because my ego doesn't want to acknowledge them, with pride on one spectrum and shame on the other keeping it in check and hidden. It's a self-regulating spectrum. But if I do, chances are, you could show me that you understand, maybe even relate at some level.

There could be feedback, self-reflection aspect to it. It's a humbling and emotional experience also because I'm taking responsibility and accountability for the wrongs and mistakes. Deep down I feel bad about them, but over time I desensitize myself because I get numb to the world with whatever attitude. If did wrong in the past, I might as well keep going as my self-worth and self-esteem is already low. I put alcohol and drugs on top of that as a bandaid and there is no telling how the day will unfold. I regret, I feel guilty, I judge myself and I mess up again because of self-sabotage.

It's a learning experience that allows oneself to be less judgemental of the mistakes which diminishes the self-critic and promotes healing. There is a cleansing part to it and allows for letting go, by relieved feelings and a release. And let's face it; it's easier to repeat what feels comfortable and normalize it over the years if it's unaddressed. Insanity becomes justified. Meanwhile, it takes a lot of work to untangle the illness and admission is the first step in order to achieve that.

Insanity is doing the same things over and over again and expecting different results and if I'm making the same mistakes all the time, I'm insane. But how do I move forward in order to strengthen my mental capacity and build character without exposing those mistakes? There is no other way to do that!

How long does it take you to get used to things you don't like?

"No one is more dangerously insane than one who is sane all the time: he is like a steel bridge without flexibility, and the order of his life is rigid and brittle"—Alan Watts

In childhood I learned to adapt to every environment whether I liked it or not. I'm like a chameleon able to take on any surroundings and find ways to cope. Often very unhealthy ways. Something which I'm working on changing now.

How long You ask? As long as it takes to make sense of it! Sometimes minutes. Sometimes days. Sometimes I accept it and sometimes I rebel. I have always been willing to go above and beyond and I cope as best as I knew how at the moment. The problem is running on the reptilian part of the brain that acts on fight-or-flight impulses, in instances where those impulses are not beneficial for survival.

CHAPTER XII- SOCIETY AND POLITICS

Why does the United States keep building prisons if they aren't effective in preventing recidivism?

"Wrongful convictions happen every week in every state in this country. And they happen for all the same reasons. Sloppy police work. Eyewitness identification is the most - is the worst type almost. Because it's wrong about half the time. Think about that"—John Grisham

Prisons are a big business in and of itself and the United States of America is the most capitalistic system in the world ever created. Free enterprise. Number of facts are the following. Prisons get paid for every prisoner housed and fed by the tax payers, which adds up. Prison corporations have or are under contracts and It's in their interest to have more people locked up since human labor also brings revenue. Prisoners provide cheap labor and get exploited in certain industries. Those policies and outlook cause overcrowded conditions too, especially at a county level. Food companies sell commissaries (food to prisoners)

Certain criminal judges have part ownership in private prisons. Politicians and business people lease lands to build more prisons on their lands and in turn get steady income out of that.Prisons also in turn, provide more jobs especially in rural places where jobs are more scarce.

Some lawyers make a killing defending people. They work with DA's, and judges. It's all about making plea deals not to overwhelm the justice system. There is a lot of money involved. I know exactly how the system works. It's a game. DA's are about statistics. Most people get intimidated into taking deals ruining their chances for better futures. They get stuck there. Politicians get elected when they say they will be tough on crime. The wheels of the criminal justice system keeps on spinning and grinding people left and right sometimes they deserve it and other times, what they need is adequate mental health instead.

The United States of America has a quarter of the world's prison population. Millions of people are locked up or on parole or probation. Like I mentioned earlier, It is a big business. Most of it drug related in my thinking. Instead of rehabilitation, the emphasis is on punishment, which clearly does not work and only marginalizes the people who suffer and are ashamed even more.

**Why has so much aggressiveness
become part of our daily lives?**

"A soft answer turns away wrath, but a harsh word stirs up anger"—Proverbs 15:1 (KJV)

This is a partial answer. First was the spoken word and the word was with God. Many causes exist why aggression has become such a part of our daily lives —the biggest one will have to be the lack of faith and fear in God and all-about-me-attitude—it destroys the world and people. Aggressiveness has always been a problem in any society because aggression is an untamed instinct that's misdirected. However, in individualistic, corporate cultures and severe hierarchical distinction delegating the workforce, it has brought unfavorable conditions because people are abusive and don't know how to relate to others.

The current structure of society arrived and as a result of shifted priorities. That's what happens when time and performance collide, meaning results. Results, results, results. The world expects to produce results. The only way results come about is by pressuring someone else to perform or managers to do that for the owners interested and driven by profits. Then, there is competition and more results required in order to remain relative.

Modern life is stressful on many fronts. Whether it be a service, industrial or entertainment sector, whoever owns the means of production, they expect results and they want to flourish. High expectations lead to low serenity and vice versa is true. Low expectations correlate with higher serenity. Life revolves around the economy. From a quick overview, it makes a lot of sense. The more collective the culture, the less innovation and more traditional . . . meaning life stays the same and the culture has much more influence over the individual unit. The more individualism and more creativity and outside the box thinking, the more wheels of the brain are turning new ideas into realities. And not always good ones either.

I suppose, the need to dominate the world and each other has many substantial benefits and perks for everyone in that society. Take the good old USA. Many complain about it, but enter the country in droves. Life becomes a bit easier here until it doesn't—when more exploitation occurs and people find out money doesn't grow on trees. It takes hard work to make it and be comfortable.

Another aspect I'd like to mention is this. Somewhere in the late 60's and early 70's, the rift between the middle class and the wealthy began to increase and the middle class shrank substantially since then. The dollar went off the gold standard and people no longer got ahead like before, while trying to live the perceptual American dream. That means global society became more and more controlled by less and fewer people, which also opened up opportunities to manipulate mass media, drive narrative, wedge between people and create more division—thus aggression.

Meanwhile, the people in power would like to stay in power and aggression is created—fear accomplishes that and keeps people in line. It involves government leaders and tycoons, or people otherwise capable of reaching a wide audience to manipulate perceptions and economy, or start new local and global conflicts —we see that all the time. The most unequal societies also tend to be the most violent. In the United States, for example, prisons comprise a quarter of the world's population as well as on various levels, prisons make money.

Next, it's no longer about order and strong values either. It's no longer about right and wrong, but about feelings, God complex and getting triggered too. It's the truth. People don't wanna hear it. (Feelings are important but they need to align with reason) People speak their own versions of truth when it suits their interests.

One example.

A pretty woman complains about equality and patriarchy and how evil the men are who objectify them. That happens until she goes to the club and gets in for free or without waiting in line because of her looks. All of a sudden, the paradigm shifts when it benefits her. This is a silly example until applied across the board. Women are no longer traditional either and gender roles are switching. That too causes conflict, aggression and tension, while universities turn out radicals when Students graduate. Life is a constant conflict. Unchecked motives lead to aggression. If a business doesn't take inventory of its stock, it goes broke.The same is with people, unfortunately.

**Who is the most dangerous person that
you have ever met or encountered?**
*"The most dangerous person is the one who
listens, thinks and observes"*—Bruce Lee

I did meet a few shiny characters of the world, but I honestly don't know who was the most dangerous one.

I know I met at least a few killers,

Scores of drug dealers,

That I suspect may have taken people's lives,
And other violent criminals.

One person admitted shooting a person in the head during an emotional retaliation. He later turned himself to the law enforcement and face the music; the drum roll of the criminal justice system—so no sense to inquire about the circumstances further. I was trying to be a bit poetic here.

How do you describe apathy?

Your life begins to end the moment you start being silent about the things that matter—Martin Luther King, Jr.

There are billions of people on the planet and millions live in apathy and are apathetic also. You got federal laws in the United States to protect eagles and turtle eggs with heavy fines when destroyed and aborting human babies wasn't a big deal until now. Worldwide there are 40 to 50 million abortions every year, with approximately 125,000 aborted babies daily.

I think we got things backwards. I know ... There are billions of us and according to some we don't deserve life. The people aborting babies in droves are the very people that weren't aborted themselves, said Ronald Reagan. How profound of a statement is that? I think that sums societal apathy pretty accurately if you ask me, providing only this one example. This is a topic without exhaustion. Let that sink in.

How do I break barriers and not accept limits?

"All kids are born geniuses, but are crushed by society"—Michio Kaku

I saw that quote recently and I thought about it.This statement makes a lot sense to me. Society puts limits on children and puts them in a box of the same, universal learning experience for the most part tells them:

"Silly, you can't discover the world. It's already been done. Get a safe job that pays bills and conform to society."

Children aren't given enough of room to explore their talents because they're pushed in a certain direction contrary to their calling. Dreams evaporate because fear is bred into them.... they're told to play it safe. Children become adults and their dreams no longer exist or linger as a wishful thinking. Fear needs to be overcome.

How can you break barriers and not accept limits?

Give yourself a worthy goal. Plot the course, direction and clear roadmap of how you're going for get there. Failure to plan is planning to fail. Be consistent and persistent. People need some goals to accomplish, bigger than

"I need to put in 20, 30, more years at my job and hopefully get a decent pension, retirement if I live to see it."

How do you break barriers?

Breaking barriers involves taking risks in life.

Playing it safe is not a definition of a Maverick—an unorthodox or independent-minded person. And if that's the case, and people are cool with it, that's okay. But if they're seeking high achievement results and want to break barriers, they gotta make something happen…stir the pot, make some commotion. Start with little things.

Afraid of flying? . . . go sky dive . . . sky is the limit . . .

Slow building of confidence because things don't happen overnight. No one can push a limit overnight. It happens in a succession of time, routine, ritual that leads to spiritual and psychic experiences combined with development of a new attitude. Depression and anxiety hinders that and many people in modern society are unfortunately stuck and hopeless and don't see the light at the end of the tunnel. Or all they see in an incoming train ready to smash them. Pushing limits is the last thing on their mind…they're struggling to survive. Modern society is Maverick's enemy. Mind over matter. You have your mind…sky is the limit…society highjacked it…work, produce, consume, be on social media for 5 hours a day, get married, have children, buy a house, get a 30 year mortgage…boom (stuck) fear, fear, fear, not all bad but it's fear inducing, it contains and limits. When things don't work out, individuals get crushed and defeated.

Maverick is a mindset set . . . the bar higher. Sure there may be some who have some kind of extraordinary experience, but I think even those, had serious struggles before it happened and they kept pushing and not giving up until it happened.

Of course having people who believe in you is probably as important as believing in yourself. They can reinforce that drive, but I don't see why strong-minded individuals can't succeed on their own...but society wants to contain...society regulates children. Adults regulate themselves and the children as part of that society. I know it's easier to write about it in simple terms, as opposed to providing some variables and complexities that go into breaking those barriers. It's always easier to intellectualize anything than actively pursuing it.

Why does it seem like humanity can't get a win lately?

"We are yet to have a conscience at all about the exploitation of human cultures"—Arthur Erickson

My thorough analysis on the current state of the world affairs and humanity reveals the following findings. The super rich are getting richer at the expense of the working class—Working harder no longer applies in the modern world. People are replaceable and abundant which diminishes their worth, with technology and innovation able to surpass an average human being without some sort of specialized expertise.

Money is being printed out of control which makes me more and more convinced the whole thing is a scam on a global scale. Now, we have to work harder for less and the wage increase doesn't account for inflation. It's a house of cards. Soon a regular home will be a million dollars and people can claim their millionaires. Too bad the money doesn't stretch as far.

Covid was made in the lab and supported by governments or certain individuals who work for government for a gain-of-function research that did what it was intended to do-—wreak havoc on the world. There are rarely any coincidences in the world and this man-made bio-terrorism is used to eliminate few people, but more importantly it's a scare tactic in which governments take more and more control and initiate restrictions.

May you *guess who isn't restricted?* Big businesses, Walmart, huge retailers, Big pharma and tech still makes a hug profit and in a few cases more than ever, but if anyone owns a restaurant or something similar, they can't operate how they would like to because of restrictions, which isn't fair at all!

Covid vaccines enrich people like Bill Gates and others who patent the vaccine formulas and make even more profit from the suffering the man-made virus created in the first place. They won't even share them with other nation states because these people don't give a thought about anybody but themselves, yet most people praise them for being great philanthropists. They have to be because it looks great, is a good PR approach and finally they're swift to write it off on taxes, and therefore it's a win for them, anyway. And TV works for them as Mr. Gates and others pay their salaries in order to spin them into angelic forces.

Here is the kick! You might not like this one, but it needs mentioning. The vaccine doesn't even work like intended and was lied about. The leaders and media said it would prevent the spread of the virus and it does no such thing. Further I will state, vaccines will cause more harm than good in the future for a variety of reasons, including blood clots that cause spontaneous deaths. Let's just say there is a lot more complaints about the side effects than media reports.

They want people to be team players and take the jab for the world's sake. Meanwhile they exploit people financially as well as by manipulation. Then Bill Gates profits and buys more arable land for food production and mor e control. We are being massively lied to and the agenda is to make most people poor and have them live in mega-cities cut out from nature and land. It's called Agenda 21. The elites want to isolate people so that humanity fear one another, while the virus never goes away. This is just a beginning. Statistics are skewed: no more flues, every death is Covid. *Now, we have to have Covid passports? What is this Nazi Germany?* Definitely heading this way and into severely dangerous territory.

People are asleep and easily manipulated through fear and intimidation and electing leaders who don't serve them like they should. Instead, these power-hungry individuals use every opportunity to instill more control, power and wealth for themselves. There are also many people who are finally waking up and seeing through the deception on the global scale. Those in charge shame people for not wearing a mask, so that when someone else sees another person not wearing theirs, they're shamed too. Anybody that had Covid, naturally has better immunity than the shot will ever provide, unless someone is compromised and elderly. And some people had Covid and knew not.

Then we have an unfavorable weather phenomenon happening with more frequency that adds to the chaos and drama of life and more misery will follow from that alone. Let me add this too. DARPA can manipulate weather if they choose to do so as well. Yes, weather like people, can also be manipulated. Technology is available and in use.

There's no incentive for the Elites to make the world a better place. If there is a lot of fear, chaos and poverty, it's easier for them to rule the world as they have for centuries and keep tabs on the population. They are the wolves keeping the sheep at bay while making themselves look like they're the saviors of the world. It takes a person able to tap into a wolf mindset to know how wolves operate. We need to start withdrawing consent. Governments work for the people, not the other way around. People have to educate themselves about the plans for the future of humankind and not believe the perpetrated all around. A wolf can smell BS from a mile away and a good wolf will warn others.

On a side note, I'm not sure if the wolf analogy works in this context.

How did people live and feel a few generations ago, when the "strong ego" was still common?

"Psychologists suggest that we must reach back at least three generations to look for clues whenever we begin untangling the emotional legacy of any one family's history"—Elizabeth Gilbert

I think in some ways people were worse off and better off too. For one thing, there was probably more bigotry and ignorance in the world. Not so much because people are better people today, but because of the world itself and how it was — rooted in deeper tradition.

Few generations ago are approximately 60, 70 years ago. The world war just ended. Western world was undergoing rapid changes on one hand while also an iron curtain in the Soviet sphere of influence and the world divided. West was afraid of the spread of communism while communism spoke of the evil capitalism. People feared nuclear apocalypse. Things were tense and people more reserved.

Many counties were, and I assume still are, exploited and people that live there too. In some way, people were limited and therefore stuck in the old ways. For example, there were fewer divorces but more spousal abuse. You heard someone got divorced back then, people were stigmatized. Someone didn't attend church services in the community; they also could have been rejected somehow. Image, image, the importance to keep up good family appearances and conservative attire prevalent.

Patriotism and pride were also engrained and military glorified until the 60s came around. People and things that didn't conform were marginalized and oppressed such as freedom to express oneself or their sexuality. More of a taboo existed and deviance punishable criminally. Homosexuality for example, was considered a mental illness in the science of psychiatry. There still exists a prevalent belief in some philosophies; the attraction is driven merely by lust of the sexual senses and perversion. Perhaps that's for another question.

But also more people were less educated with less access to improving themselves. They had no social media, fewer ways to learn from others, limited to newspapers, schools, authority guidance and therefore certain narrative.

In other ways, people were more real too I believe. They had stronger family ties and values, not distracted and bombarded by the external stimulus of cell phones and access to the mass media at the scale we have experienced today. I'm sure there is a likelihood of mass manipulation now, as it was back then too and much more misinformation, disinformation that leads to even more confusion.

However, I believe because we have more access to the world, even digitally, individuals have more opportunities to learn, heal and understand another and see through the ego. Ego that is concerned with self and driven by many forms of fear and dis-eases evident in the world today. But it's also easier for the ego to medicate itself with an excess of unhealthy doses of distorted reality.

I think ego is very strong today as well. Society has become more narcissistic and self-obsessed. High pace life is confusing and leaves true relationships stranded. Ego is open to abundance of superficiality, compulsion to addictions such as online pornography and online gaming that devours people's lives and frying their brains, with constant dopamine hits among the more notorious modern phenomena. Women opt out of relationships, LGBT community imposes its will on the society and underage castrations are normalized. I believe there is much more mental illness happening at this time then ever before and these are quite alarming to me. The ego is too willful and deceived and many people turned their backs to God.

How are we always basically in "survival mode" even when we think we are not, and why is this true?

"Princes and governments are far more dangerous than other elements within society"—Niccolo Machiavelli

I don't know or think most people are always in the survival mode. I think people mistake survival mode with running upsetting thoughts and feelings, fears and traumas, could be a survival mode, but I don't think it's continuous. The limits haven't been pushed, social contract upheld in most cases. Once that goes and enough of time passes to adjust.

What can I say- Free Americana- anything goes for many characters, without some internal guide that separate the boundaries before they blur and morality no longer applies. In a way society is heading that way and people allow it. There is an agenda taking place and people who don't have God create their own religious-like causes; environment, feminism, Black Lives Matter, Antifa. These are not creative but destructive forces.

I know for me, if I was in a survival mode, my outlook on things would look a bit more chaotic and uncertain. I'm talking survival mode:

people are out to kill you, you fend for yourself, you lack proper housing, shelter, food and may be somewhere outdoors, dealing with unpleasant elements both with regards to weather and society. That alone affects people in a variety of ways, I imagine, and survival mode is a prerogative, a top plate agenda. Armageddon, forced labor camps, no food on the shelves, public executions, no law and order, homelessness, true poverty, heavy addictions, religious persecutions, gang violence, sex trafficking, murders, tortures...

That's a survival mode . . . Many people already live in these conditions and while some have no clue about it, it wouldn't take long to experience under the formation of the right circumstances. Right now for a lot of people refrigerator lies seven feet away and an ice-cream in a freezer ready to quell upsetting emotions. And I don't want to sound mean or demeaning but, whoever is not in this mess, has a chance to HEAL

CHAPTER XIII - TIPS FOR LIVING

What is the best way to live safely?

"Live life to the fullest. You have to color outside the lines once in a while if you want to make your life a masterpiece. Laugh some every day. Keep growing, keep dreaming, keep following your heart. The important thing is not to stop questioning"—Albert Einstein

From my own experiences, I can say there aren't best and safe ways to approaching life. Life happens and people can't always control outcomes because there are too many factors and variants involved. And they shouldn't try to control everything in the first place.

I probably made more than my share of acceptable mistakes, so I can't really give advice on safe ways to approaching life, but to live as best as possible with emphasis on growing through the process.

What will help is surrounding oneself with people who are about change and success. Success in life and success in relationships. I think that's the key. Good support system and good friendships are more important than anything else, because people are the biggest resource and asset in life.

Having a lifetime partner based on merit and compatibility is a lot more important than based on physical and sexual attraction too...Often that's lust talking, not love. Best if one could have both, but many people make a mistake in that department alone and choose a wrong partner with unintended consequences and a world of pain afterwards.

My one friend: married a woman and she manipulated him to the point of siphoning business money into a separate account. Beautiful woman with a rotten personality. A few other people I know became divorce and things didn't work out, at least for one of the two. We're talking serious heartache and suffering and the children that have no say regarding the matter. They struggle the most long term.

If one was to be safe in approaching life, I'd seek safety and cautious in choosing an adequate lifetime partner, because life can become miserable real quick when the honeymoon phase disappears. Then again. As people change for the better, the also change for the worse. Change goes both ways. So the right partner today is no longer applies tomorrow or true colors reveal the hr masterpiece.

What are your short rules for a better life?

"You just try to take it one day at a time . . . You

> *step on the basketball floor and just play. It's fun. I'm comfortable with it"*—Kobe Bryant

Live through this day only but be better than yesterday and look with hope on tomorrow. Try not to regulate anyone but myself and accept the world as is because it is and I'm powerless over many things while working on changing what I can change— namely myself. I wouldn't write they are rules but something I'm striving for.

CHAPTER XIV - TECHNIQUES AND COPING SKILLS

How do I stop feeling scared? What are some calming techniques?

"Fear is the path to the dark side. Fear leads to anger. Anger leads to hate. Hate leads to suffering"—Yoda

There are a variety of things you can do to curb or diminish your fears and you ought to find something that works especially for you. Therefore, I have included few things that I have done, do, or experimented with during the times of distress. Hope that helps.

Focusing on breathing is a good distraction from scary feelings. Mindful breathing has a very calming effect after few minutes. You could practice that every day, multiple times a day so that in times of fear this is the go to technique. Sit down close your eyes and take deep, controlled breaths while counting to ten.

You could also focus on something in the room or whatever place you're in and think about its external look. Describe

what you see.

It could be the same thing for any object in your hand, even as trivial as a tea cup. You could for instance, describe its feel, texture, color and anything else you see to distract yourself from scary feeling. Meanwhile you could drink a nice cup of hot and soothing herbal tea to help quell scary feelings and emotions. I used to drink a decent amount sleepy time tea even in the morning, instead of a stimulating coffee and it helped with the anxieties.

Short repeated prayers settle fearful feelings and nerves as well, as I have found out during distressing times. These are of great benefit as well and will get your mind away from fearful thoughts.

 Self soothing, calming talk can help you as well.
Everything is alright, I'm safe
This is going to pass

Enjoyable activity for distraction and mood elevation such as reading something that gives you comfort and solace

Exercise is great for fearful feelings to get rid of that anxiety and fear and elevate the brain with feel-good chemicals.

Journaling is another great way to let this thoughts and feelings go. As you empty your head from all the fears, they tend to lose their power and grip while you distract yourself. You can write exactly what you're going through and write positive, encouraging statements.

In a time of distress you could call a friend or a family member and talk to them. Even if they don't pick up you can leave a message and describe what you're going through. If they're you good friend, they won't judge you for that. Of course, noteworthy is a therapy if possible. Talking about these things help as well as you hearing yourself talking and getting a feedback, while listening to the therapist about your fears even if the don't plaque you at the moment, they lose their power later on.

Calming music or meditation music and also meditating too. There is a variety of ways to do that. I will not get into details but, there is plenty of info out there regarding how people meditate. Some focus on the breath alone and others repeat a mantra or a certain sound.

Another coping technique is not over doing things in life. It is important not to over stimulate the mind with frightening news or social media a negative posts, memes and such. It's very wise to stay away from negative and fearful content and people alike.

If getting adequate sleep is difficult or falling asleep is hard, try taking a hot shower or a bath. This initially causes the body and head temperature to increase. Later, as the head cools down, it activates more chemicals responsible for getting tired and sleepy. The head needs to cool down a couple of degrees in order for a person to fall asleep.

That's one important hack and technique to implement to fall asleep faster. One of the most and undervalued things to feel well and balanced is proper rest and sleep. Not enough can be said about sleep as lack of it has a tendency to disregulate all the bodily and mind functions. Good, regular sleep hygiene is critical to operating properly on a daily basis.

What is a useful life hack you can learn in five minutes?

"Give yourself a gift of five minutes of contemplation in awe of everything you see around you. Go outside and turn your attention to the many miracles around you. This five-minute-a-day regimen of appreciation and gratitude will help you to focus your life in awe"—Wayne Dyer

Practicing mindful breathing and meditation is where it's at. Everything starts and ends with breath including life. Mindfulness is powerful but coupled with a five minute meditation everyday to start can make a huge difference in people's lives. People learn to sit with their discomfort and feelings without distracting with other means. This increases a person grip and handle on their emotions and disciplines them.

Self awareness in life is the key. Enlightenment is the path to gratitude and humility which comes and goes as the door of self-will takes over to numb, medicate and distract oneself with anything in the physical. Mindfulness, breathing and meditation counters the escape when things begin to feel uncomfortable. Spoken by a person addicted to more and who always looked to fill in the void which nothing could fill. It got deeper. Today I go deeper into a rabbit hole but instead of getting stuck, I am mining gold—meaning self-improvement, we-improvement.

REFERENCES

Mayo clinic online- Definition of Personality Disorder

The lived experience of recovery in borderline personality disorder: a qualitative study by Fiona Y. Y. Michelle L. Townsend, Caitlin E. Miller, Mahlie Jewell and Brin F. S. Grenyer, 2019

Online resources

Personal experiences

ABOUT THE AUTHOR

Gtstarr

Graduated with a B.A in Psychology. GTStarr is passionate and actively engaged in mental health recovery on a group level. He also enjoys learning about humanities. His interest lie in research and writing in fields related to the psychology of the 

mind, cognition, behavior and emotions, as well as, faith based studies and much more. In addition, he is actively pursuing a writing career.

BOOKS BY THIS AUTHOR

Seesaw Derangement

Psychological fiction novel about an addict in jail struggling with life.

Poems Of The Addicted

Poems written over the years. They relate to addiction, recovery and difficulties. Some are part of the author's creativity.

Twelve Steps In A Nutshell: Workbook

Workook designed to help individuals overcome character defects and addictions. It contains multitude of questions and worksheets dealing with recovery and Higher Power as a source of strength that heals and grows